BUILD-A-LAB!
SCIENCE EXPERIMENTS

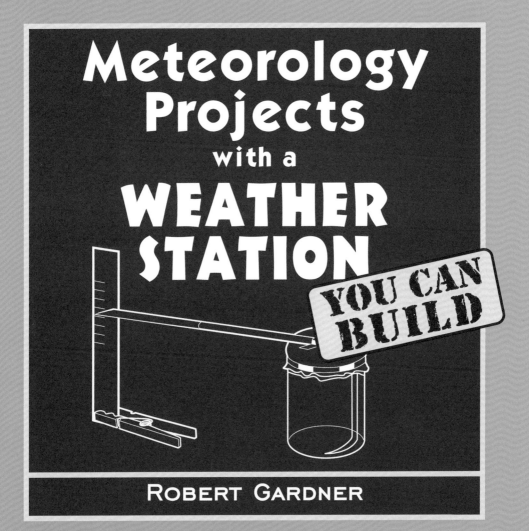

Meteorology Projects
with a
WEATHER STATION

YOU CAN BUILD

ROBERT GARDNER

Enslow Publishers, Inc.
40 Industrial Road
Box 398
Berkeley Heights, NJ 07922
USA

http://www.enslow.com

Library of Congress Cataloging-in-Publication Data

Gardner, Robert, 1929–
    Meteorology projects with a weather station you can build / by Robert Gardner.
        p. cm. — (Build-a-lab! Science experiments)
    Summary: "Presents meteorology experiments using a weather station that the reader builds"—Provided by publisher.
    Includes bibliographical references and index.
    ISBN-13: 978-0-7660-2807-4
    ISBN-10: 0-7660-2807-0
    1. Meteorology—Experiments—Juvenile literature. 2. Meteorological stations—Experiments—Juvenile literature. 3. Science projects—Juvenile literature. I. Title.
QC863.5.G366 2008
551.5078—dc22

                              2007010614

Printed in the United States of America

10 9 8 7 6 5 4 3 2 1

To Our Readers: We have done our best to make sure all Internet Addresses in this book were active and appropriate when we went to press. However, the author and the publisher have no control over and assume no liability for the material available on those Internet sites or on other Web sites they may link to. Any comments or suggestions can be sent by e-mail to comments@enslow.com or to the address on the back cover.

Illustration credits: Jonathan Moreno

Photo credits: Enslow Publishers, Inc.

Front Cover: Jonathan Moreno (blueprint), Shutterstock (cloud, lightning, sun, weather vane)

CONTENTS

EXPERIMENTS WITH A 🎖 SYMBOL FEATURE IDEAS FOR YOUR SCIENCE FAIR.

CONTENTS

INTRODUCTION

You can build your own weather station. Once it is built, you can use it to collect the information that weather scientists or meteorologists use to predict the weather. The instruments you will build can also be used to do experiments. The experiments will help you learn the science needed to understand weather. By using your weather station and doing experiments, you will learn how clouds form, why the wind blows, how to predict tomorrow's weather, how gases are causing global warming, and much more.

Most of the materials you will need to build a weather station and do the projects and experiments in this book can be found in your home. Several experiments may require things that you can buy in a supermarket, a hobby or toy shop, a hardware store, or one of the science supply companies listed in the appendix. Some may call for items that you might borrow from your school's science department.

Occasionally, you will need someone to help you with an experiment that requires more than one pair of hands. It would be best if you work with friends or adults who enjoy experimenting as much as you do. Then you will both enjoy what you are doing. **The instructions in this book will let you know if any danger is involved in doing an experiment. In some cases, to avoid any danger to you, you will be asked to work with an adult. Please do so.** We do not want you to take any chances that could lead to injury.

Like any good scientist, you will find it useful to record your ideas, notes, weather data, and anything you can conclude from your experiments and weather records in a notebook. By so doing, you can keep track of the information you gather and any conclusions you reach. And you can refer back to experiments you have done, to help you with future projects.

You will not be the first person to track the weather. George Washington and Thomas Jefferson, our country's first and third presidents, kept detailed weather records. But it was not until after messages could be sent long distances by telegraph in the 1840s that it became possible to track storms moving across the country. Today, satellites orbiting Earth give us weather data on a worldwide basis. Computers have made it possible to make scientific models of storms. These models help meteorologists as they forecast weather.

SCIENCE FAIRS

The projects in this book marked with 🏅 include ideas for a science fair. These ideas may be useful in preparing for your next science fair. However, judges at such fairs do not reward projects or experiments that are simply copied from a book. For example, a fluffy cotton model of a cloud would probably not impress judges. A report of an experiment to explain how raindrops form in a cloud would receive much more consideration than pieces of cotton glued to a blue background.

Science fair judges tend to reward creative thought and imagination. However, it is difficult to be creative or imaginative unless you are really interested in your project, so choose something that appeals to you. Consider, too, your own ability and the cost of materials needed for the project.

If you decide to use a project or idea found in this book for a science fair, you will need to find ways to modify or expand the project. This should not be difficult because as you do these projects, new ideas for experiments will come to mind. These new experiments could make excellent science fair projects because they spring from your own mind and are interesting to you.

If you decide to enter a science fair and have never done so before, you should read one or more of the books listed in the Further Reading section. Some of these books are about science fairs. Those books will provide helpful hints and useful information. They will show you how to avoid the pitfalls that sometimes confront first-time entrants. You will learn how to prepare winning reports that include charts and graphs, how to set up and display your work, how to present your project, and how to talk to judges and visitors.

THE SCIENTIFIC METHOD

When you do a science project, especially one with your original research, you will need to use what is commonly called the scientific method. In many textbooks you will find a section devoted to this subject. They will probably tell you that the scientific method consists of a series of steps.

The idea that there is a scientific method probably came about because of the way scientists report their findings. All good scientific projects try to answer a question, such as "Does wind travel in a straight line?" Once you have a question, you will need to form a hypothesis. A hypothesis is an idea of what you think will happen. Your experiment should then test your hypothesis.

Scientific reports are very similar in format and include the problem, the hypothesis, the experimental procedure, the results, and a conclusion. You should follow a similar format when you prepare the report for your project.

SAFETY FIRST

Most of the projects included in this book are perfectly safe. However, the following safety rules are well worth reading before you start any project.

1. Do any experiments or projects, whether from this book or of your own design, under the supervision of a science teacher or other knowledgeable adult.

2. Read all instructions carefully before proceeding with a project. If you have questions, check with your supervisor before going any further.

3. Maintain a serious attitude while conducting experiments. Fooling around can be dangerous to you and to others.

4. Wear approved safety goggles when doing anything that might injure your eyes.

5. Do not eat or drink while experimenting.

6. Have a first aid kit nearby while you are experimenting.

7. Never experiment with household electricity except under the supervision of a knowledgeable adult.

8. Do not touch a lit high-wattage bulb. Also, never let water droplets come in contact with a hot light bulb. Light bulbs produce light, but they also produce heat and will shatter if suddenly cooled.

9. Never look directly at the sun. It can cause permanent damage to your eyes.

10. The liquid in some thermometers is mercury, a dense liquid metal. It is dangerous to touch mercury or breathe mercury vapor, and such thermometers have been banned in many states. When doing your experiments, use only non-mercury thermometers, such as those filled with alcohol. If you have a mercury thermometer in the house, **ask an adult** if it can be taken to a local mercury thermometer exchange location.

11. Practice patience as you experiment. Experiments performed with care lead to results in which you can have confidence.

BUILD YOUR OWN WEATHER STATION

Meteorologists, people who study and forecast weather, use many instruments to make measurements that help them study weather and predict it. You can build a weather station that will contain many of the instruments that meteorologists use.

Weather takes place outdoors. Therefore, many of the instruments you build and use will have to be placed outside. Once you have built your instruments and understand how they work and what they measure, you can use them to learn about weather. You will also use them to do the many experiments found in this book. Experimenting gives you a hands-on understanding of weather, which is more fun and more interesting than just reading about it.

The instruments you will need in your weather station are a thermometer to measure temperatures, a barometer to measure air pressure, a rain gauge to measure precipitation (rain and snow), a wind vane to find wind direction, a device to measure wind speed, and a hygrometer to measure relative humidity. Later, you will also discover a way to find dew points and calculate absolute humidity. The difference between relative and absolute humidity will be discussed at that time. You can begin by doing an experiment to see how a thermometer works.

To see how a thermometer works, you can make a simple one.

1. To begin, add a drop or two of food coloring to a test tube or bottle.

2. Completely fill the test tube or bottle with water.

3. Put one end of a clear drinking straw or a length of glass tubing into the water. Leave most of the straw or tubing above the water.

4. Surround the straw or tubing with a modeling-clay plug at the point where it enters the test tube. The clay should cover and fill the test tube opening. It should fit snugly around the straw or glass so that air cannot enter or leave the test tube or bottle.

5. Push the clay plug firmly into the mouth of the test

You Will Need

- **large test tube or narrow-neck bottle**
- **food coloring**
- **water**
- **clear drinking straw or glass tube**
- **modeling clay**
- **2 drinking glasses**
- **marking pen**
- **hot and cold tap water**
- **ruler**

tube. The water should rise about halfway up the drinking straw, as shown in Figure 1.

6. Put the test tube in an empty drinking glass so it will stay upright. Leave it for ten minutes so the water can reach room temperature. Then mark the water level on the straw or tubing with a marking pen.

7. Put the test tube in a glass of hot tap water. What happens to the water level in the straw or tubing? Use the marking pen to mark this new level.

8. Put the test tube in a glass filled with cold water. What happens to the water level in the straw or tubing? Use the marking pen to mark this new level. What happens to

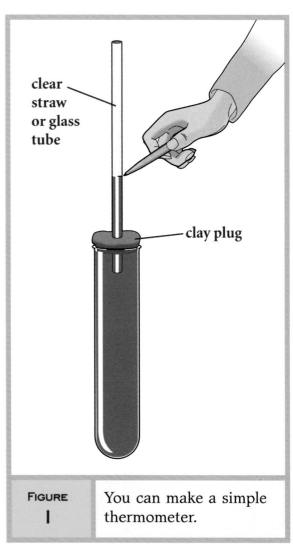

clear straw or glass tube

clay plug

FIGURE 1

You can make a simple thermometer.

the volume of water (the amount of space it takes up) when it gets hotter? When it gets colder?

Use a ruler and marking pen to divide the space between your two new marks into equal parts. Each part is one degree. You can number the degrees and name your new temperature scale after yourself!

Two common temperature scales are named for the scientists who made them. Both scientists used two fixed temperatures (temperatures that are always about the same) in making their scales. Daniel Gabriel Fahrenheit (1686–1736) used the freezing temperature of a salt solution and human body temperature to mark low and high points on his scale. Anders Celsius (1701–1744) used the freezing and boiling points of water to mark points on his scale. He divided his scale into 100 degrees between the low and high points.

IDEA FOR A SCIENCE FAIR

Carry out an experiment to show what happens to the volume of air when it is heated or cooled. Use what you learn to make an air thermometer.

A THERMOMETER FOR YOUR WEATHER STATION

The simple thermometer you made in the previous experiment showed you how a thermometer works. But it is not a very practical instrument. It would not work at temperatures below 0°C (32°F) because the water would freeze. Also, the temperature scale you invented is not familiar to others. You can use any household alcohol thermometer to measure temperature. **Do not use thermometers that contain mercury!** (See the Safety First section in the introduction.) It would be nice to have a thermometer that measures and stores the maximum (high) and minimum (low) temperatures each day. It would also be helpful to have a thermometer with both Fahrenheit and Celsius scales. However, any household alcohol thermometer will do.

To see that the thermometer behaves like the one you made in Experiment 1-1, place your finger on the

You Will Need

- **household alcohol thermometer, preferably one with both Fahrenheit and Celsius scales that measures and stores maximum and minimum temperatures on a daily basis**

thermometer bulb. What happens to the liquid inside the narrow tube? What happens to the liquid if you hold an ice cube against the thermometer bulb?

The thermometer will be used to measure air temperature. It should be placed outdoors in a protected area that is shaded. A thermometer in sunlight will show a temperature higher than the temperature of the air.

IDEA FOR A SCIENCE FAIR

Measure and record the high and low temperature each day for all four seasons. Calculate the average high and low temperatures for each season. Then calculate the temperature range (from low to high) for each season.

AIR PRESSURE

We live at the bottom of a sea of air that is more than 60 miles (100 km) deep. Most of the air is within 6 miles (10 km) of Earth's surface. Like everything else, air is subject to Earth's gravity because air has mass.

1. To see that air has mass, let the air out of a basketball or soccer ball, but do not squeeze it. Let the ball keep its round shape.

- **AN ADULT**
- **basketball or soccer ball**
- **laboratory balance**
- **air pump**
- **empty one-gallon metal can**
- **dish soap**
- **water**
- **oven mitts**
- **stove or hot plate**
- **insulated mat or some newspapers**
- **can's screw-on top or rubber stopper that fits can's opening**
- **test tube or vial**
- **paper towel**
- **sink**

2. Weigh the ball on a laboratory balance. Record the mass.

3. Next, pump air into the ball until it is very hard. Then weigh the ball again. Record its mass when inflated. How can you tell that air has mass?

   Because air has mass, it pushes on everything

it touches. This push is called pressure. Pressure is the push (force) that something exerts on the area that it touches. When you stand on a floor, the pressure you exert on the floor is the Earth's gravity pulling on you, spread over the area of the soles of your feet.

To see the effect of air pressure, find an empty one-gallon metal can that was used to hold food. Clean its inside thoroughly with dish soap and water. Then pour half a cup of water into the can. Leave the can uncovered.

Ask an adult wearing oven mitts to put the can on a stove burner or hot plate. Let the water in the can boil for several minutes. Steam will fill the can and push out the air. **Have the adult** quickly place the can on an insulated mat or some newspapers. **The adult** should then immediately screw the cover back on the can or plug its opening with a rubber stopper. The steam, which has replaced the air in the can, will condense as it cools. This will reduce the pressure inside the can, creating a partial vacuum. Watch carefully for several minutes. What happens as the pressure of the air outside the can becomes much greater than the pressure inside the can?

Here is another way to see that air exerts pressure. Fill a

test tube or vial with water. Cover the mouth of the tube or vial with a small piece of paper towel. Turn the vessel upside down over a sink. You will find that air pressure on the piece of towel keeps the water in the tube or vial.

With all that pressure from the air, why doesn't your body collapse in the same way the can did? The reason is that the pressure inside your body is the same as the pressure of the air.

IDEA FOR A SCIENCE FAIR

Design a model to show why air moves in and out of our lungs when we breathe.

AIR PRESSURE, WEATHER, AND A BAROMETER

Weather takes place in Earth's atmosphere. In fact, most of what we consider weather takes place in the troposphere, the 6-mile– (10-kilometer–) deep air closest to Earth's surface (Figure 2a). This thin slice of atmosphere is only about 0.15 percent of Earth's diameter. But the troposphere is where we find clouds, rain, snow, sleet, hail, lightning, and all other weather phenomena.

a)

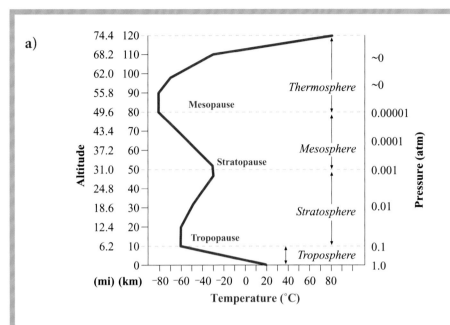

b) Torricelli's barometer

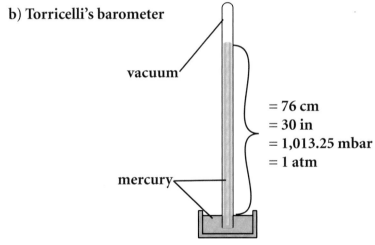

vacuum

= 76 cm
= 30 in
= 1,013.25 mbar
= 1 atm

mercury

FIGURE 2

a) The layers of the atmosphere are defined by meteorologists. Pressure and temperature change at increasing altitudes.
b) A pressure of one atmosphere (atm) is equal to 76 cm of mercury or 1,013.25 millibars (mbar).

Air pressure is a big part of weather and weather predictions. Consequently, your weather station should have an instrument that measures air pressure. That instrument is a barometer. It measures the weight of a column of air extending from Earth's surface to the top of the atmosphere. At sea level, that weight is equal to the weight of a similar column of water 10 meters (33 feet) deep.

The world's first barometer (see Figure 2b) was invented by Evangelista Torricelli (1608–1647), an Italian physicist. Torricelli filled a narrow 1.2-meter– (4-foot–) long glass tube with mercury. He put his thumb over the tube's open end (the other end was sealed) and inverted it. He then placed the thumb-covered end in a dish of mercury and removed his thumb. The mercury began to empty into the dish, but it stopped when the mercury level in the tube was 76 cm (30 in) above the mercury in the dish. This left an empty space at the top of the tube. Torricelli reasoned that the empty space was truly empty, a vacuum, because no air bubbles had come up the tube. He also reasoned that the pressure due to the weight of the mercury pushing downward at the mouth of the tube was balanced by the pressure of the air pushing against the mercury in the dish. (Air exerts pressure in all directions—up, down, and sideways.)

Meteorologists still measure air pressure by the height of mercury in a Torricelli barometer. A mercury height of 76.0 cm (29.9 in) is normal air pressure at sea level. And we often say that air pressure at sea level is 76.0 cm (29.9 in) of mercury.

However, pressure is defined as a force acting on an area, a force per area (F/A). Can the height of a mercury column be expressed as a force per area? The answer is yes.

The force that a mercury column exerts on the open end of a Torricelli barometer is its weight. (An object's weight is just the pull of Earth's gravity on the object's mass.) As for the area, it is equal to the size of the barometer's open end. Dividing the force by the area yields a pressure of 1,013.25 millibars (mbar). Millibars are often used by meteorologists to express air pressure.

Torricelli used a mercury barometer. However, you will use a different kind of barometer (an aneroid barometer) because mercury is poisonous.

A BAROMETER FOR YOUR WEATHER STATION

1. **Use scissors to cut off the neck of a balloon.**

2. Slip the rest of the balloon over the opening of a wide-mouth jar or a drinking glass. Secure it to the jar or glass with a strong rubber band.

3. Put two drinking straws together to make one straw. Use scissors to cut one end of the straw diagonally to make a pointer, as shown in Figure 3a.

4. Using clear tape, tape the other end of the straw to the center of the rubber balloon covering the jar or glass.

5. Finally, use a strip of cardboard, clothespins, ruler, and marking pen to make a scale with lines 0.5 cm apart. Place the scale beside the end of the pointer, as shown in Figure 3a.

You Will Need

- **scissors**
- **balloon**
- **wide-mouth jar or drinking glass**
- **strong rubber band**
- **2 drinking straws**
- **clear tape**
- **cardboard**
- **clothespins**
- **ruler**
- **marking pen**
- **notebook**
- **empty one-liter plastic soda bottle**
- **hot water**
- **refrigerator**
- **aneroid barometer**

a) A HOMEMADE BAROMETER

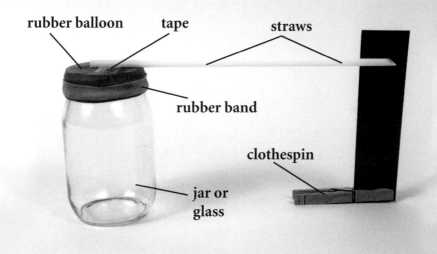

rubber balloon   tape   straws

rubber band

clothespin

jar or
glass

b) AN ANEROID BAROMETER

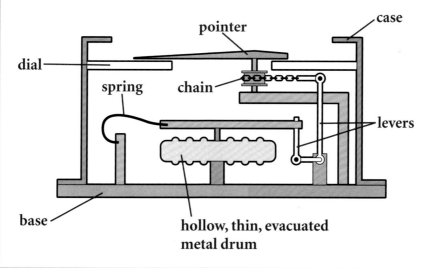

case

pointer

dial

spring   chain

levers

base

hollow, thin, evacuated
metal drum

| FIGURE 3 | a) A homemade barometer. b) An aneroid barometer. |

6. Record the position of the pointer in your notebook. Look at the position of the pointer every few hours for the next few days. Be sure to look when the weather is changing from clear to stormy, or vice versa. What do you notice?

   The balloon barometer you have built will indicate changes in air pressure. As the air pressure increases, the rubber surface is pushed down and the pointer goes up. When the air pressure decreases, the higher pressure under the rubber surface pushes it upward and the pointer moves down.

   However, for this barometer to be useful, it must be kept at a constant temperature.

7. To see why, pull the mouth of a balloon over the top of an empty one-liter plastic soda bottle.

8. Then hold the bottle under hot running water. What happens to the volume of the air in the bottle when its temperature rises? How can you tell?

9. Next, place the bottle and attached balloon in a refrigerator. What happens to the volume of the air when its temperature decreases? How can you tell?

   Why would your homemade barometer have to be kept at a constant temperature to measure air pressure?

The other problem with the barometer you made is that it can tell you only when air pressure is increasing or decreasing. It can't use a numerical measurement, like centimeters of mercury or millibars, to tell you what the pressure is.

An aneroid barometer is based on the same principle as the one you made. However, look carefully at the diagram in Figure 3b. The thin, hollow metal drum, which corresponds to the jar or glass that you used, does not contain air. It is empty—a vacuum. Consequently, the drum's surface will only move in or out in response to pressure. It contains no air that would expand or shrink depending on temperature.

You may have an aneroid barometer in your home. Sometimes you will find such a barometer together with a thermometer and a hygrometer (see Experiment 1-9). If not, you can buy an aneroid barometer at a hardware store or at one of the science supply houses listed in the appendix.

You can keep the barometer indoors. The air pressure indoors is the same as the pressure outdoors. No building is airtight. If the air pressure outside increases, air will move into your home until the two pressures are equal. If the air pressure outside decreases, air will move out of your home.

AIR PRESSURE AND ALTITUDE

As you go up into the atmosphere, there is less air above you. Therefore, you might expect air pressure to decrease as altitude increases.

To see if this is true, take your aneroid barometer to the basement of a building. If possible, choose a building with three or more levels (a skyscraper would be ideal).

1. Read the barometer carefully and record the air pressure. Then carry the barometer to the top floor of the building. Again, read the barometer carefully and record the air pressure. Does the air pressure decrease as you go higher?

2. Carry the barometer up a tall hill. Does the air pressure decrease at the top of the hill?

3. Take the barometer on an automobile ride. Compare air pressures at the top and bottom of hills or mountains. Does air pressure decrease with altitude?

You Will Need

- **aneroid barometer**
- **tall building**
- **notebook**
- **pen or pencil**
- **hill**
- **automobile**
- **unopened bag of potato chips**

4. You might also take along an unopened bag of potato chips on one of your up and down journeys or on an airplane trip. Feel the bag at low and high altitudes. What do you notice about the bag's firmness at the different altitudes? Can you explain what you observe?

IDEAS FOR A SCIENCE FAIR

*   Measure air pressure at different altitudes. Plot a graph of air pressure versus altitude. How can you use air pressure to measure altitude?

*   Find the number of home runs hit in various major league ballparks. Would you expect there to be any relationship between home runs hit and the altitude of the ballpark? Is there any relationship?

A Rain Gauge

Rain is measured by the depth of the water it produces in inches or centimeters.

1. You will need a clear glass or plastic jar with straight sides (Figure 4). An olive jar works well.

2. Place the jar in an open area away from buildings, trees, and anything that might prevent rain from falling into it. You could **ask an adult** to wrap wire from a coat hanger around and under the jar to act as a holder. The end of the wire could be made into a hook, and you could hang the rain gauge from a fence. You might tape the jar to a stake. You could **ask an adult** to drill a shallow hole slightly

You Will Need

- **AN ADULT**
- **clear glass or plastic jar with straight sides, such as an olive jar**
- **wire coat hanger**
- **tape**
- **stake**
- **drill and bit (optional)**
- **ruler**
- **clear ruler (optional)**
- **marking pen**
- **notebook**
- **local newspaper**
- **tall coffee can**

larger than the jar's diameter in the top of a post. The jar could be set in the opening.

3. After a rainfall, you can use a ruler to measure the depth of the water in the jar, or you can tape a clear ruler to the jar's side. You might put a strip of tape on the side of the jar. You could then mark a scale on the tape with lines 1/4 in or 0.5 cm apart.

4. After measuring the rainfall, record your measurement, empty the jar, and replace it. You can compare your measurement of rainfall with one found in your local newspaper.

   Rainfall is important. Too much rain can cause flooding and too little rain can result in a drought. Rain seeps into the soil and enters the water in the ground, known as the aquifer, or runs off into a stream or river.

   Snow can be measured as rainfall, but an inch of snow usually contains much less water than an inch of rain.

5. To convert snowfall to inches of water, first measure the depth of the snow.

6. Next, fill a tall coffee can with loose snow. Do not pack the snow. Bring the can inside and let the snow melt.

7. Measure the depth of the can and the depth of the water

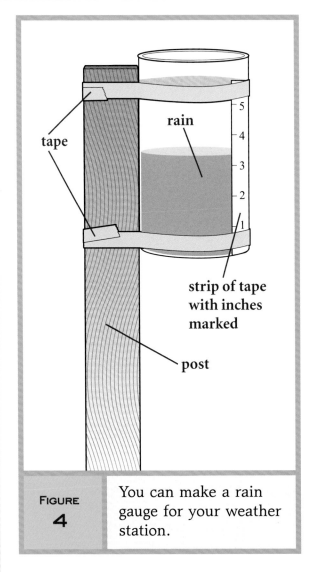

tape

rain

5

4

3

2

1

strip of tape
with inches
marked

post

FIGURE
4

You can make a rain
gauge for your weather
station.

(melted snow). From the ratio of depth of snow to depth of water, you can figure out the equivalent amount of rainfall delivered by the snow. For example, if the can was 12 inches high and the melted snow was 1 inch deep, then a 2-foot snowfall brought the equivalent of 2 inches of rain.

Don't expect the same ratio of snow depth to inches of rain to be true of all snowfalls. Two feet of light fluffy snow might equal an inch of rain. On the other hand, a few inches of wet slushy snow might also provide an inch of rain.

You can build a wind vane** that will tell you the direction of the wind. Wind direction is defined as the direction from which the wind is coming. A north wind comes from the north. If you face north, the wind will blow against your face.

Wind vanes are sometimes called weather vanes because changes in the wind direction can often indicate a change of weather. As you observe the weather and record data provided by the instruments in your weather station, you will discover how changes in the direction of the wind can help you predict weather.

Your wind measuring device should be placed as high as possible in an open

You Will Need

- **AN ADULT** !
- **piece of soft wood about 1 ft (30 cm) long, 1 in (2.5 cm) wide, and 1/2 in (1.3 cm) thick**
- **saw with a thin blade, such as a hacksaw**
- **heavy-duty aluminum pie or baking pans**
- **shears**
- **drill and bit**
- **finishing nail**
- **post**
- **plastic washer**
- **ribbon**
- **thumb tack**
- **small stones**
- **measuring tape**

area away from buildings, trees, and anything that might prevent wind from reaching it. (Official winds are taken at a height of 10 meters, but you do not need to be "official.")

1. To make a wind vane, **ask an adult** to cut a piece of soft wood approximately 1 ft (30 cm) long, 1 in (2.5 cm) wide, and 1/2 in (1.3 cm) thick.

2. At each end of the stick, **have the adult** use a saw with a thin blade, such as a hacksaw, to cut a 1/2 in– (1.3 cm–) long slit. The head and tail of the wind vane's arrow will be slid into these slits and glued.

3. The vane's head and tail can be made from heavy-duty aluminum pie or baking pans. The tail should be a trapezoid about 3 in (8 cm) wide, 7 in (18 cm) long on one side, and 4 in (10 cm) long on the side that slides into the slot. (See Figure 5.) The head of the arrow-shaped wind vane can be a triangle with a base of 3 in (7.5 cm) and an altitude of the same length. The wide end of the arrow should be slid into the other slit that was cut in the wooden shaft, as shown in Figure 5.

4. Balance the arrow on your finger. **Ask an adult** to drill a hole through the shaft at the balancing point. The hole should be

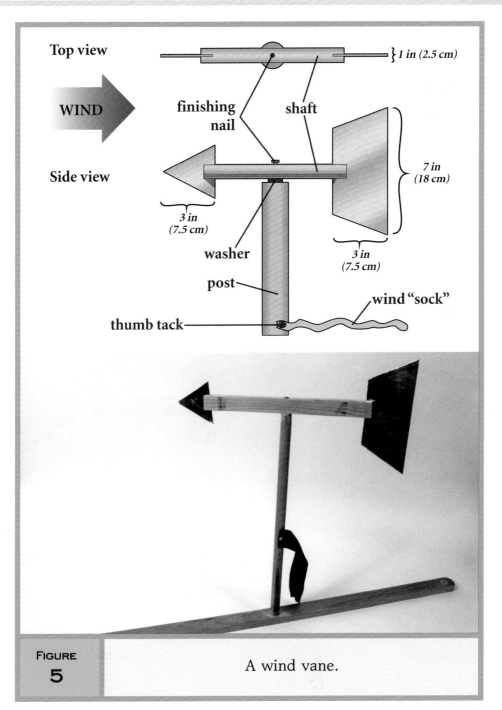

Top view

WIND

finishing nail

shaft

} 1 in (2.5 cm)

Side view

7 in (18 cm)

3 in (7.5 cm)

washer

3 in (7.5 cm)

post

wind "sock"

thumb tack

FIGURE
5

A wind vane.

slightly wider than the diameter of the finishing nail you will use to fasten the weather vane to a post.

5. Place a plastic washer between the shaft and the post to which it will be nailed.

6. A finishing nail can be used to attach the weather vane to a tall post. Put the nail through the hole in the shaft and the washer. Then hammer the nail into the post. Leave a space between the nail head and the shaft so that the shaft is free to turn.

7. Tack a piece of ribbon to the post. The ribbon can serve as a wind sock like those used at small airports. The wind sock will also detect the wind's direction. In fact, it may detect winds that are too light to move the wind vane. How can you tell the direction of the wind by looking at the wind sock?

GETTING DIRECTIONS

Stand at the post on which the wind vane is mounted. If you can point to all the main directions (north, south, east, and west), you can easily determine the direction of the wind. If you don't know the directions, here's a way to find north.

In the Northern Hemisphere, it is easy to find north, the direction toward the North Pole. All you need to do is find the shortest shadow of the post on which the wind vane is mounted. The shortest shadow of the post will occur at midday, when the sun is highest in the sky and directly south. But midday is seldom at noon. The sun knows nothing about the clocks we use to tell time. Your best bet is to start marking the end of the post's shadow as the sun approaches its midpoint in the sky. You can mark the post's shrinking shadow by placing small stones at the end of each shadow. Continue to do this at five or ten minute intervals. Stop when the shadow starts growing longer. Think of the mark that indicates the end of the shortest shadow as an arrow head. Think of the post as the tail of the arrow. The "arrow" points toward the north.

Knowing north, you can identify all the other directions. Just face north, and south will be behind you; east will be on your right, and west will be on your left. You can easily find the wind direction by looking at the wind vane and the wind sock.

AN INSTRUMENT TO MEASURE WIND SPEED

Meteorologists use an anemometer to measure wind speed. This instrument has three cups that catch the wind and rotate. The anemometer's spinning shaft turns a small generator that sends an electric current to the meter dial inside the station. The faster the wind, the greater the current.

You Will Need

- **AN ADULT** (!)
- **piece of wood about 6 in (15 cm) square**
- **safety glasses**

- **hammer**
- **nails**
- **heavy gloves**
- **tin snips**
- **tall tin can**
- **pliers**
- **car**
- **road with little traffic**
- **marking pen**
- **Beaufort Scale (Table 1)**

You can make a different kind of instrument to measure wind speed.

1. You will need a piece of wood about 6 in (15 cm) square, as shown in Figure 6.

2. **Put on safety glasses.** Then hammer nails partway into two corners of the wood.

3. **Ask an adult wearing**

heavy gloves to use tin snips to cut a strip of metal from a tall tin can. The strip should be about 1 in (2.5 cm) wide and about 8 in (20 cm) long. The adult can use pliers to bend one end of the strip loosely around a nail, as shown in Figure 6. When you hold the instrument upright, as shown, the free end of the strip should rest on the other nail. A mark at the lower end of the strip can indicate a wind speed of zero.

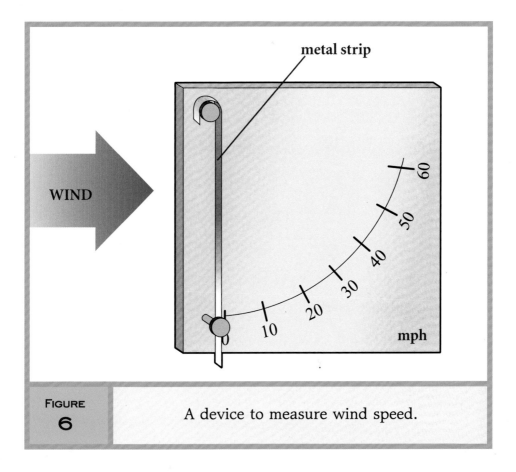

| FIGURE 6 | A device to measure wind speed. |

When the wind meter is pointed into the wind, the strip will be blown up at an angle.

4. To calibrate your wind meter you will need a car, a calm day (little wind), and **an adult driver**. Find a straight road where there is very little traffic. Ask your driver to go exactly 10 miles per hour (16 kph). Hold the wind meter out the window so that the air pushes the metal strip away from the nail. Make another mark on the wood at the lower end of the metal strip. This mark can later be labeled 10 mph (16 kph).

5. In the same way, make other lines when the car is traveling 20 mph (32 kph), 30 mph (48 kph), and 40 mph (65 kph).

6. Test your wind meter on the next windy day by holding it so the wind pushes the metal flap. How much does the wind speed change from one minute to the next?

The Beaufort Scale is another way to measure wind speed. It was devised by Sir Francis Beaufort (1774–1857), a hydrographer in the British navy. This scale allows you to determine wind speed by observing things in the wind. Compare measurements on your wind meter with the Beaufort Scale shown in Table 1, on pages 41–42.

TABLE I	The Beaufort Scale			
Beaufort Number	**Wind**	**Wind Speed**		**Visual Observations**
		(mph)	**(kph)**	
0	calm	0	0	Smoke rises vertically.
1	light air	1–3	2–5	Wind direction is given by smoke but not by wind vane.
2	light breeze	4–7	6–12	Leaves rustle; wind vane moves; wind can be felt on your face.
3	gentle breeze	8–12	13–19	Wind extends small flags; leaves are in constant motion.
4	moderate breeze	13–18	20–29	Small branches move; dust and loose paper are lifted.
5	fresh breeze	19–24	30–38	Small trees with leaves sway; wavelets form on lakes.

TABLE I	The Beaufort Scale			

Beaufort Number	Wind	Wind Speed		Visual Observations
		(mph)	(kph)	
6	strong breeze	25–31	39–50	Large branches move; utility lines seem to whistle.
7	near gale	32–38	51–61	Large trees sway; walking into wind is a bit difficult.
8	gale	39–46	62–74	Twigs break off trees; it is difficult to walk against wind.
9	strong gale	47–54	75–86	Buildings sustain slight damage.
10	storm	55–63	87–101	Trees are uprooted; buildings sustain considerable damage.
11	violent storm	64–74	102–118	Widespread damage is seen.
12	hurricane	75+	118+	There is extreme destruction of property.

A Hygrometer to Measure Relative Humidity

Humidity has to do with the amount of water vapor (gaseous water) in the air. Absolute humidity measures the mass of water in a cubic meter of air. It is expressed in grams per cubic meter (g/m^3). You will measure absolute humidity in Chapter 2.

Relative humidity is expressed as a percentage. It compares the amount of moisture (water vapor) in the air to the amount of moisture needed to condense into dew or a cloud. But more moisture can mix with warm air before it condenses than with cold air. Consequently, the relative humidity might be 90 percent in the early morning when the air is cold, and drop to 40 percent by afternoon when the air is warmer. The air over a desert is generally very dry

You Will Need

- **two identical household alcohol thermometers**
- **milk carton**
- **rubber bands or tape**
- **scissors**
- **shoelace**
- **water**
- **cardboard**
- **notebook**
- **pen or pencil**
- **Table 2**

and the relative humidity may be less than 10 percent. On the other hand, a rain forest is very damp and the humidity might be 100 percent.

To measure relative humidity, we make use of the fact that evaporation has a cooling effect. When your sweat evaporates, it cools your skin. It prevents your body temperature from rising. To see this effect on a dry day or in an air-conditioned room, wet the end of your finger with your tongue. Then dampen your cheek by rubbing your finger across it. You will immediately feel a cooling effect as the moisture evaporates.

The drier (less humid) the air, the faster water evaporates and the greater its cooling effect. Meteorologists have used this fact to devise a way to measure relative humidity. They use a wet-and-dry-bulb hygrometer, which consists of two thermometers. This instrument is also known as a psychrometer. One thermometer bulb is kept dry. It measures the temperature of the air. The second thermometer bulb is kept moist so that water evaporates and cools it. From the air temperature and the difference between the wet bulb and dry bulb temperatures, the relative humidity can be determined. This is done by using the information in Table 2. Of course, if the two thermometers have the same temperature, there is no net evaporation. This means water is condensing as fast as it evaporates, so the relative humidity is 100 percent.

1. To build your hygrometer, find two household alcohol thermometers that read the same temperature when placed side by side. Attach the thermometers to a milk carton using rubber bands or tape, as shown in Figure 7.

2. Cut a piece of shoelace about 6 in (15 cm) long. Slip the open end over one thermometer bulb.

3. Use scissors to make a hole in the carton near the shoelace. Push the shoelace through the hole so that it rests on the bottom of the carton. Add water to the carton so that the shoelace gets wet. Water will travel up the shoelace by capillary action. This will keep the bulb wet so that it will be cooled as water evaporates.

4. To use your hygrometer to measure humidity, fan the wet bulb for five minutes with a piece of cardboard. Then quickly read the temperatures on both thermometers. Record the temperatures in your notebook. Subtract the wet bulb

TABLE 2	Finding the Relative Humidity (Percent) Using Fahrenheit Temperatures																				
Dry bulb Temperature in °F	Temperature Difference in °F (Dry Bulb Temperature – Wet Bulb Temperature)																				
	1	2	3	4	5	6	7	8	9	10	11	12	13	14	15	16	17	18	19	20	25
35	91	81	72	63	54	45	36	27	19	10											
40	92	83	75	68	60	52	45	37	29	22	15										
45	93	86	78	71	64	57	51	44	38	31	25	18	12								
50	93	87	80	74	67	61	55	49	43	38	32	27	21	16	10						
55	94	88	82	76	70	65	59	54	49	43	38	33	28	23	19	14					
60	94	89	83	78	73	68	63	58	53	48	44	39	35	31	27	24	20	16	12		
65	95	90	85	80	75	70	66	61	56	52	48	44	39	35	31	27	24	20	16	12	
70	95	90	86	81	77	72	68	64	59	55	51	48	44	40	36	33	29	25	22	19	
75	96	91	86	82	78	74	70	66	62	58	54	51	47	44	40	37	34	30	27	24	
80	96	91	87	83	79	75	72	68	64	61	57	54	50	47	44	41	38	35	32	29	15
85	96	92	88	84	80	76	73	69	66	62	59	56	52	49	46	43	41	38	35	32	20
90	96	92	89	85	81	78	74	71	68	65	61	58	55	52	49	47	44	41	39	36	24
95	96	93	89	85	82	79	75	72	69	66	63	60	57	54	51	49	46	43	41	38	27

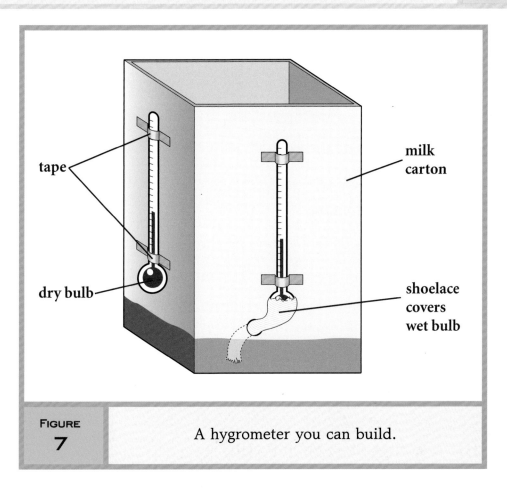

tape

milk
carton

dry bulb

shoelace
covers
wet bulb

FIGURE

7

A hygrometer you can build.

temperature reading from the dry bulb temperature reading
to find the difference between the two.

5. Use Table 2 to find the relative humidity. First, find the temperature closest to the dry bulb temperature at the left side
of the table. Next, find the number at the top of the table that
matches the temperature difference between the wet bulb
and dry bulb thermometers.

The relative humidity (percentage) is found where the dry bulb temperature row intersects the temperature difference column. For example, if the dry bulb temperature is 60°F (15.6°C) and the wet bulb temperature is 50°F (10°C), then the temperature difference is 10°F and the relative humidity is 48 percent.

If you own or buy a sling psychrometer, you will find it quite easy to measure relative humidity on a daily basis. Simply spin the wet and dry bulb thermometers until the wet bulb thermometer temperature is steady. Then read both thermometers to find the temperature difference, and consult Table 2.

IDEA FOR A SCIENCE FAIR

If you have curly or wavy hair, you know that humidity affects human hair. Use that fact to build a hair hygrometer from a long strand of clean human hair. You can also calibrate the hygrometer. To get 100 percent humidity, place your hair hygrometer in the bathroom while you take a hot shower. To get approximately zero percent humidity, blow air over it with a hair dryer set on cool.

WEATHER DATA AND CLOUDS

Now that you have a weather station, you can begin collecting data. The data will help you see how your instruments and observations can be used to predict the weather. In addition to collecting data, you will investigate and make use of a number of other things.

You will learn about dew points, which can become part of your daily weather data. You will find out how to measure both absolute and relative humidity and how wind chill temperatures are measured. All these measurements can be used to help you make weather predictions. You will also make a cloud, see how clouds can help you predict the weather, investigate how temperature affects evaporation, and learn more about thunderstorms.

COLLECTING WEATHER DATA

At least once a day, **more often if possible,** record the data your instruments provide. Use a table like the one shown below. You can keep the tables in a notebook. You will find it useful to refer to and review the data frequently.

Date	Temperature		Humidity (%)	Rain or Snow (in)	Air Pressure (in)	Wind Direction	Wind Speed	Dew Point
	High	Low						

The last column in the table requires some explanation. In the next experiment, you will learn how to find dew points. Dew points are especially useful to have during warm weather.

As you record data, preferably at the same time each day, you will find it helpful to make notes. Your notes might include interesting observations that prove useful in making predictions about the weather. For example, you might note that a drop in air pressure was followed by damp or rainy weather, or that increasing air pressure was

You Will Need

- **weather instruments in your weather station**
- **notebook**
- **pen or pencil**

followed by fair skies. You might also notice that changes in the wind's direction or speed are linked to certain weather changes. You may find that the types of clouds you see can be used to predict the weather. Later in this chapter, you will learn about cloud types and their significance.

If you like, you can use symbols like those used by meteorologists when you record notes and data. The symbols used by many meteorologists are found in Figure 8.

ABSOLUTE HUMIDITY AND DEW POINTS

There is moisture (water vapor) in the air. That moisture is our source of rain. Only so much water can exist as vapor at a given temperature. Sometimes air is saturated with water vapor. This happens when the amount of water condensing from the air equals the amount evaporating into the air. But unless it is raining, the air is not usually saturated.

The actual amount of water vapor in a given volume is the absolute humidity. As you learned in Chapter 1, the relative humidity is the ratio of the moisture in the air to the total amount that could be mixed with air at a given temperature.

/////	Showers	○	Clear
⚡⚡	Thundershowers	●	Overcast
🌢🌢	Rain	◑	1/2 cloud cover
✳ ✳ ✳	Snow	◕	3/4 cloud cover
— — —	Ice	◔	1/4 cloud cover
★ ★ ★	Flurries	(H)	High pressure system
		(L)	Low pressure system

FIGURE 8	Some common meteorology symbols.

TABLE 3	The Maximum Amount of Water Vapor, in Grams, That Can Be Found in a Cubic Meter at Different Temperatures		
Temperature		Maximum Mass of Water Vapor (g)	
(°F)	(°C)		
32	0	4.8	
41	5	6.8	
50	10	9.3	
59	15	12.7	
68	20	17.1	
77	25	22.8	
86	30	30.0	
95	35	39.2	

The maximum mass of water vapor in a cubic meter at different temperatures is given by the data in Table 3.

You can use the information in Table 3 to find the absolute humidity. But to do so, you must first find the dew point.

MEASURING DEW POINTS

1. **Add warm or hot water** to a shiny metal can until it is at least half full.

2. Take the can and water outside. If moisture (dew) immediately appears on the can, use warmer water.

3. Place a thermometer in the water. Use the thermometer to stir the water as you add small pieces of ice.

4. Watch the outside surface of the can. When you first see dew forming on the can, read the thermometer and record the temperature. That temperature is the dew point.

5. Knowing the dew point, you can find the absolute humidity.

You Will Need

- **warm or hot water**

- **shiny metal can**

- **thermometer**

- **small pieces of ice**

- **Table 3**

- **notebook**

- **pen or pencil**

Suppose you find the dew point to be 59°F (15°C). From Table 3, you see that a cubic meter of air at 59°F is saturated when it contains 12.7 g of water vapor. Therefore, the absolute humidity is 12.7 g/m^3.

If the temperature of the air is 77°F (25°C), you

can see from Table 3 that 22.8 g/m³ would be needed to saturate the air. Consequently, the relative humidity is:

$$12.7 \text{ g/m}^3 \div 22.8 \text{ g/m}^3 = 0.56 = 56\%$$

But suppose the dew point is at some temperature not listed in the table, such as 53°F. No problem! Use the data in Table 3 and the graph in Figure 9. The graph lets you interpolate between the plotted points. For example, if the dew point is 53°F, the graph indicates that at 53°F,

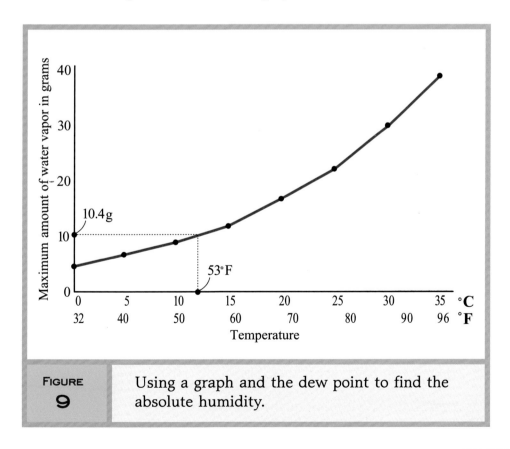

FIGURE	Using a graph and the dew point to find the
9	absolute humidity.

the maximum amount of water in a cubic meter of air is approximately 10.4 g/m^3.

What is the temperature of the air where you are measuring the dew point?

6. Using the air temperature and the dew point, find the relative humidity. How does the relative humidity based on your dew point measurement and Table 3 compare with the reading according to your hygrometer?

How does the humidity inside a building compare with the humidity outside?

During which season of the year does the absolute humidity tend to be highest? When is it lowest? When is the relative humidity highest? Lowest? During which season of the year is the air driest inside your home or school? Under what conditions are you unable to determine the dew point?

Weather reports always give the dew point, so you can obtain it from those for your weather notebook. However, you should measure the dew point occasionally, especially when the air feels very dry or very damp. Then compare your measurement with that of the weather report.

IDEAS FOR A SCIENCE FAIR

- Do an experiment to show why you should use a metal container rather than a plastic or glass one to find the dew point.

- Research how the data in Table 3 was obtained.

- Add crushed ice to the can you used in Experiment 2-2 until it is about one-third full. Add an equal volume of table salt and stir to mix the salt and ice thoroughly. Place a thermometer in the salt-ice mixture. Watch the side of the can very carefully. Do you see frost collecting? Do you first see dew that freezes, or does the frost form without first becoming a liquid (dew)? What have you learned about the formation of frost?

A WEATHER FORECAST BASED ON DEW POINTS

If you measure dew points frequently in the summer, you can issue a weather report about air comfort. When dew points reach 70°F, the humid air feels oppressive. Dew points between 60°F and 70°F cause many people to feel uncomfortable even when temperatures are in the 60s or 70s. Air with a dew point below 60°F is generally considered comfortable.

EASY-TO-MAKE PREDICTIONS

Here's an hour-by-hour summer weather report you can make. By measuring temperature and humidity and referring to Table 4 (The Heat Index), you can estimate how the weather will feel to people in terms of temperature.

Read down the left-hand column until you reach the relative humidity measurement you made. Then read across the top row until you come to the actual air temperature. Run your finger down that column until you reach the row that contains the relative humidity on the left-hand side. The temperature you find in that column will tell you how warm the air actually feels to the average person. When the heat index reaches 105°F, sunstroke and heat exhaustion are likely.

After recording the humidity and air temperature, refer to Table 4. You can then tell how high the temperature will feel. From the table, you can see that low humidity may cause people to feel that it is cooler

You Will Need

- **thermometer**
- **hygrometer**
- **Tables 4 and 5**
- **wind speed instrument**

TABLE 4	The Heat Index									
Relative Humidity (percent)	**Air Temperature (°F)**									
	70	75	80	85	90	95	100	105	110	115	120
	What the Temperature Feels Like (°F)									
10	65	70	75	80	85	90	95	100	105	111	116
20	66	72	77	82	87	93	99	105	112	120	130
30	67	73	78	84	90	96	104	113	123	135	148
40	68	74	79	86	93	101	110	123	137	151	
50	69	75	81	88	96	107	120	135	150		
60	70	76	82	90	100	114	132	149			
70	70	77	85	93	106	124	144				
80	71	78	86	97	113	136					
90	71	79	88	102	122						
100	72	80	91	108							

than the actual temperature. On the other hand, with high humidity, people will feel it is warmer than their thermometers indicate.

Your winter weather forecast might include estimates of how cold the air will feel because of the wind speed. After recording the wind speed according to your wind speed meter or Beaufort scale, you can estimate how cold it will feel outdoors. To do this, read the wind chill temperature in Table 5. This chart shows how wind speed affects the way the temperature feels. The top line shows the actual air temperature in °F. The vertical column on the left gives the wind speed up to 40 mph. For example, with a wind speed of 20 mph and an air temperature of 0°F, the wind chill (the way the temperature feels) is −22°F.

If the wind chill temperature is −19°F or lower, frostbite can occur in 15 minutes or less. Such wind chill temperatures lead meteorologists to issue a winter weather warning about the danger of frostbite. Wind speeds greater than 40 mph have little additional effect on the way the temperature feels.

TABLE 5	Wind Chill											
Wind Speed (mph)	**Air Temperature (°F)**											
	40	30	20	10	5	0	–5	–10	–15	–20	–25	–30
	How Air Temperature Feels Due to Wind (°F)											
calm	40	30	20	10	5	0	–5	–10	–15	–20	–25	–30
5	36	25	13	1	–5	–11	–16	–22	–28	–34	–40	–46
10	34	21	9	–4	–10	–16	–22	–28	–35	–41	–47	–53
15	32	19	6	–7	–13	–19	–26	–32	–39	–45	–51	–58
20	30	17	4	–9	–15	–22	–29	–35	–42	–48	–55	–61
25	29	16	3	–11	–17	–24	–31	–37	–44	–51	–58	–64
30	28	15	1	–12	–19	–26	–33	–39	–46	–53	–60	–67
35	28	14	0	–14	–21	–27	–34	–41	–48	–55	–62	–69
40	27	13	–1	–15	–22	–29	–36	–43	–50	–57	–64	–71

MAKING A CLOUD

Clouds are the source of the rain that gives life to plants and animals. Clouds are also useful, as you will discover, in making weather predictions.

You may have accidentally made a cloud by opening a can or bottle of cold soda on a hot day. The cloud probably appeared briefly just above the bottle's opening.

You can make a cloud quite easily any time you want.

1. Remove any paper from the outside of a clear, empty 2-liter plastic soda bottle.

2. Pour about half a cup of warm water into the bottle.

3. Screw on the cap and shake the bottle to saturate the air inside with water vapor.

4. Hold the bottle up against a light background such as a window.

5. Shake the bottle again. Then squeeze and release it. You will probably not see a cloud

You Will Need

- **AN ADULT**
- **light background such as a window**
- **clear, empty 2-liter plastic soda bottle with screw on cap**
- **warm water**
- **matches**
- **table salt (sodium chloride)**
- **glass of ginger ale**
- **2-liter bottle of diet cola**
- **mint Mentos candy**

because one ingredient is missing—condensation nuclei. (You will learn more about condensation nuclei in Experiment 2-5.)

6. **Ask an adult** to light a match, blow it out, and quickly drop the match into the bottle. There are now smoke particles inside the bottle.

7. Quickly recap it. Shake the bottle again and hold it up against a light background. Squeeze it to increase the pressure inside the bottle. Then suddenly release your squeeze. This will decrease the pressure inside the bottle, allowing the air and water vapor to expand. You should see a cloud form.

8. To see another example of the effect of condensation nuclei, add salt crystals to a glass of ginger ale. Watch a trail of gas bubbles form as the salt falls through the liquid. The crystals act as condensation nuclei for the gas bubbles in the ginger ale.

9. For a spectacular example of gas forming on condensation nuclei, take a 2-liter bottle of diet cola outside. Drop some mint Mentos candy into the bottle and stand back to avoid being hit by the geyser!

IDEA FOR A SCIENCE FAIR

Design an experiment to measure the size of raindrops. Does the size of the drops change as a storm advances?

TEMPERATURE OF AN EXPANDING GAS

In the previous experiment you suddenly decreased the pressure on moist air by releasing your squeeze on the bottle. When air rises, its pressure decreases. This should not surprise you. You found it to be true when you did Experiment 1-5. When the pressure on any gas decreases, it expands. Does anything else happen when a gas expands?

1. To find out, hold a thermometer about a foot from the nozzle of a spray can. One that sprays air freshener works well. The can should have been in the room for at least ten minutes, so that its contents are at room temperature. The vapor within the can is under pressure. It will expand when released.

2. Record the air temperature. Then press the nozzle so that the expanding vapor strikes

You Will Need

- **thermometer**
- **spray can (an air freshener can works well)**
- **notebook**
- **pen or pencil**
- **metal jar lid**
- **clear plastic container that can be sealed**
- **table salt (sodium chloride)**
- **warm water**

the thermometer bulb. What happens to the temperature? What happens to the temperature of a gas when it expands?

You learned in Experiment 2-4 that moisture and cooling by expansion are not the only things needed for cloud formation. The water vapor needs condensation nuclei on which to condense (change from a gas to a liquid). Without nuclei on which to condense, water vapor can cool to temperatures as low as –40°F (–40°C) without condensing.

You used smoke particles. In nature, smoke works but is not essential. Instead, many tiny salt crystals are carried into the air by updrafts when ocean waves break as they strike shore. The crystals are only about one ten thousandth of a millimeter in diameter (0.0001 mm). But you can use crystals of a visible size to see what happens in a cloud.

3. Sprinkle a few crystals of table salt (sodium chloride) on the top of the metal jar lid. Place the lid on the bottom of the clear plastic container.

4. Pour only enough warm water into the container to cover the bottom. Then seal the container. The water will evaporate, filling the container with water vapor.

5. After about fifteen minutes, open the container and look at

the salt crystals. Notice that they have been replaced by tiny hemispheres of water. The salt particles served as nuclei on which the vapor condensed.

6. If the air is dry, you can remove the metal lid and watch the salt crystals reform, as the water in which they are dissolved evaporates.

    If the air in a cloud is very cold, the drops can freeze into small ice crystals that may grow bigger through collisions with smaller nearby droplets. Falling through the bottom of the cloud, the ice crystals can melt into raindrops or fall as snowflakes. Whether it is rain or snow depends on the air temperature.

IDEAS FOR A SCIENCE FAIR

*   Design and carry out an experiment to detect the tiny particles found in air. Then develop a way to find the number of particles per cubic yard or meter.

*   You can capture and preserve snowflakes. You can then examine them under a microscope. Place some microscope slides on a thin sheet of wood, such as a shingle. Put them in a cold protected place that is below 32°F (0°C). Put a spray

can of clear Krylon lacquer in the same cold place. Once the slides and lacquer are cold, spray a thin coat of lacquer on each slide. Hold the wood sheet with the slides in the falling snow until a few flakes collect on each slide. Put the slides back in the same cold place overnight so the lacquer can dry. Take the slides out of the cold and examine them under a microscope. What additional experiments can you do using this technique?

"RAIN" FROM WATER VAPOR

A water cycle exists in nature. Water evaporates into the air. As it rises and expands, it cools. Eventually, water vapor may cool enough to condense (change to a liquid) on condensation nuclei.

You can make it rain in your kitchen. Here's how!

1. Fill an aluminum pie pan with ice cubes.

2. Add hot water to a large, clear glass jar until it is about two-thirds full.

3. Put the pan of ice cubes on the open top of the glass jar.

4. After about fifteen minutes, look at the inside sides of the jar. What do you see? Watch carefully for a few minutes. You may see drops of "rain" falling from the bottom of the pan into the jar. Or you may see drops of "rain" from the pan run down the side of the jar.

You Will Need

- **aluminum pie pan**
- **ice cubes**
- **large (one-quart) clear glass jar**
- **hot water**

5. Carefully lift the pan of ice. What do you see on the bottom of the pan?

How is your experiment similar to the way real rain is made? How is it different?

Some of the hot water in the jar changed to a gas. We say it evaporated. Water that has changed to a gas is water vapor. When the water vapor touched the cold pan, it condensed (changed back to a liquid). The condensed water formed drops. Some drops became so big they probably fell back into the jar. This is similar to what happens in clouds. Clouds are actually made up of tiny water drops. The drops form when water vapor cools and condenses. If the drops grow bigger, they may fall as rain.

TYPES OF CLOUDS

Meteorologists classify clouds into three main types: cirrus, cumulus, and stratus. Clouds were given Latin names in 1803 by Luke Howard, an Englishman who watched clouds as a hobby. He later added another type—nimbus (from the Latin word for rain cloud).

Cirrus (from the Latin word for curl) clouds are thin, curly, and wispy in appearance. They are sometimes called "mares' tails."

Cumulus (from the Latin word for heap) clouds are the

white, puffy, lumpy, fair-weather clouds commonly seen on warm summer days.

Stratus (from the Latin word meaning stretch out) clouds are thin and layered. They often blanket the entire sky. Fog is a stratus cloud at ground level.

Today, meteorologists use three prefixes to classify clouds according to their height. The prefix *cirro–* means high clouds at altitudes greater than 20,000 ft (6,100 m). *Alto–* indicates clouds at middle altitudes of 6,500 to 20,000 ft (2,000 to 6,100 m). *Strato–* means low-altitude clouds, from ground level (as in fog) to 6,500 ft (2,000 m).

Using these names, you can arrive at the basic types of clouds found in Figure 10 and Table 6.

Cirrostratus clouds are thin and sheetlike, and may cover the entire sky. Sunlight or moonlight shines through these clouds. The light may cause halos to form around the sun and moon. Cirrocumulus clouds are patches or sheets of white puffy or lumpy clouds.

Altocumulus clouds are like cirrocumulus clouds but appear bigger because they are lower and therefore closer to

FIGURE 10 — Ten types of clouds.

TABLE 6	Types of Clouds, Their Appearance, and the Approximate Heights at Which They Are Found		
Type	**Appearance**	**Height**	
		meters	**feet**
cirrus	thin, wispy, feathery	>6,000	>20,000
cirrostratus	layered, rain may follow	>6,000	>20,000
cirrocumulus	puffy, lumpy, fair weather	>6,000	>20,000
altostratus	layered, rain-producing	2,000–6,000	6,500–20,000
altocumulus	puffy, lumpy, fair weather	2,000–6,000	6,500–20,000
stratus	layered, rain-producing	0–2,000	0–6,500
nimbostratus	dark, layered, rain-producing	0–2,000	0–6,500
stratocumulus	puffy, lumpy, often in dark patches	0–2,000	0–6,500
cumulus	puffy, lumpy, fair weather	low–2,000	low–6,500
cumulonimbus	puffy, lumpy, rain (thunderstorms)	low–12,000	low to 70,000

you. Altostratus clouds are gray or whitish sheets that cover the sky. A dim sun can be seen through these clouds.

Nimbostratus clouds cover the sky with a heavy dark gray layer. Stratocumulus clouds cover the sky with a deep, dark, and puffy gray layer. Cumulonimbus clouds are cumulus clouds that grow upward. They can become thunderstorm clouds and acquire an anvil shape at great heights.

Of course, you may see more than one type of cloud in the sky at the same time. On a lovely August day, you may see cirrus and cirrocumulus clouds at a high altitude and puffy cumulus clouds closer to the ground.

EFFECT OF TEMPERATURE ON EVAPORATION

The moisture in the atmosphere, and therefore the rain that falls, comes from water that evaporates from oceans, lakes, and other places, including damp earth. How does temperature affect evaporation? You can find out.

1. Fill one glass with cold water and ice cubes. Fill another glass with hot tap water at about 105°F (40°C).

You Will Need

- **AN ADULT** **(!)**
- **2 glasses**
- **cold water**
- **ice cubes**
- **hot water**
- **metric measuring cup or graduated cylinder**
- **2 aluminum pie pans about 5 in × 3 in × 2 in deep**
- **hot plate, food warmer, or stove**
- **thermometer**
- **clock or watch**

2. Pour 100 mL of the cold water (no ice) into a metric measuring cup or graduated cylinder. Empty the 100 mL into one of two aluminum pans. Set the pan aside.

3. Measure out 100 mL of the hot water and pour it into an identical pan. **Ask an adult** to place this pan on a hot plate, food warmer, or

stove. Adjust the heat to keep the water at about 105°F (40°C).

4. After an hour, bend one corner of the pan holding the cold water to make a pouring spout. Do the same to the other pan.

5. Measure the volume of cold water that remains by pouring the water into a graduated cylinder or measuring cup.

6. Then measure the volume of hot water that remains.

How much cold water evaporated? How much hot water evaporated? How does temperature affect the rate at which water evaporates? How do you think warmer oceans would affect global rainfall?

THUNDERSTORMS

Thunderstorms are common on warm, humid summer days. The warm moist air rises, often pushed upward by another air mass. As it expands and cools, the water vapor condenses into a cumulus cloud. The heat produced by condensation warms the air, adding fuel to the updraft and causing the cloud to grow taller. Often the cloud takes the shape of an anvil (an upside-down triangle) as its temperature becomes equal to the temperature of the air above it.

As the cumulus cloud grows into a cumulonimbus cloud, strong updrafts keep raindrops from falling. Bouncing about in the updraft gives the drops time to grow larger. Eventually the rising air currents can no longer support the weight of the large drops. They begin to fall, but as they do, they evaporate. This has a cooling effect, making the air denser, so it begins to fall. This results in downdrafts that eliminate the humid updrafts, thereby cutting off the needed "fuel" supply. The storm destroys itself.

As you know, thunderstorms are accompanied by booming noises (thunder). For reasons not well understood, the top of a cumulonimbus cloud becomes positively charged while the lower side becomes negatively charged. Meteorologists do know that ice particles are necessary for electrical charging to take place. If the electrical potential energy becomes very large, charges (lightning) flow across the cloud. Lightning can also travel from cloud to ground. Charges on the ground are attracted to opposite charges at the base of a cloud. Consequently, tall objects are more likely to be struck by lightning because they are closer to the charged clouds. There is no limit to the number of times they can be struck.

Thunder is heard shortly after the lightning. The air around the lightning bolt is heated to temperatures as high as 54,000°F (30,000°C). The heated air expands suddenly, creating sound waves.

Sound travels at about 0.2 miles per second, while light travels at 186,000 miles per second. How can you use these different speeds to measure the distance from you to a lightning strike?

SOME WEATHER SCIENCE

Meteorologists are well trained in science. They have to study physics, chemistry, geology, and biology in order to understand and forecast weather. If you are considering meteorology as a career, plan on taking many science courses. You cannot understand weather without a firm foundation in science. So as you continue to collect weather data, you can also learn about the science involved in weather.

This chapter provides a glimpse of the role science plays in understanding weather. You will find out what causes air to move and create winds, and how to find the causes. You will carry out experiments to see the effect of the spinning Earth on moving air masses. You will also discover how heat affects air and what causes air to rise or sink. You will read about air masses and weather fronts. Finally, you will learn about the jet streams and how to read weather maps.

WHAT CAUSES WIND?

Wind is the movement of air over Earth's surface. For anything to move, a force must act on it. You can discover the force that causes air to move.

1. Fill a balloon with air. Squeeze the neck of the balloon to seal it. With your other hand, feel the balloon's surface. Do you feel an opposing force? Is the pressure greater inside or outside the balloon?

2. Hold the mouth of the balloon near your face. Then slightly release your grip on the balloon's neck. Can you feel a wind moving against your face? Why do you think air is flowing out of the balloon?

SUN, PRESSURE, AND WIND

As you have just seen, winds are caused by air that is pushed from high pressure to low pressure. But why are there differences in pressure? The reason is that the sun's heat is not spread uniformly across Earth's surface. Tropical regions receive much more heat than polar regions; consequently, tropical air is much warmer than polar air.

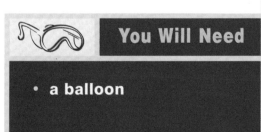

You Will Need

- **a balloon**

As you will learn later in this chapter, warm air becomes less dense (lighter) and so exerts less pressure. Higher pressure air then moves into the region of lower pressure.

If we lived on a frictionless planet that did not rotate, pressure differences alone could account for wind speed and direction. However, we live on Earth, a planet that turns and where friction is common. As a result, there is more to wind than just pressure differences.

If you give a ball a push, it moves. But the ball slows down and eventually stops because of friction. Friction is a force that opposes motion. Friction between the ball and the surface over which it rolls acts against the ball's motion. Friction acts against you when you try to push a box along a floor. Air moving over the earth rubs against trees, grass, water, buildings, and so on. The air's velocity, like that of a rolling ball, is reduced by friction.

In addition to pressure and friction, there is something else that affects winds. It is known as the Coriolis [cor ee OH lihs] effect; it is caused by Earth's rotation. It was discovered in 1835 by the French physicist Gaspard-Gustave de Coriolis (1792–1843).

To understand this effect, think about the ground at the North Pole.

You Will Need

- **ball**
- **shears or scissors**
- **cardboard**
- **turntable, piano stool that can spin, or lazy susan**
- **tape**
- **felt-tip pen**
- **a partner**
- **ruler or yardstick**

It simply turns in place. It has no speed. However, at the equator, the ground moves from west to east at a great speed. The equator is 24,900 miles (40,086 km) long, and the Earth turns once every 24 hours. Therefore, anything on the equator moves eastward at 1,038 mi/hr (1670 km/hr) because:

$$\frac{24{,}900 \text{ mi}}{24 \text{ hr}} = 1{,}038 \text{ mi/hr} \quad \text{or} \quad \frac{40{,}086 \text{ km}}{24 \text{ hr}} = 1{,}670 \text{ km/hr}$$

Because of this rotation of the Earth, wind does not move in a straight line over its surface.

You can get a hands-on feeling for the Coriolis effect by doing an experiment.

1. Cut a piece of cardboard to match the circular top of a turntable, a piano stool that can spin, or a lazy susan. Tape the cardboard to the surface on which you place it. The center of the cardboard represents Earth's North Pole; its circumference represents Earth's equator.

2. Use a moving felt-tip pen to represent the path of wind moving from the North Pole toward the equator. Draw a straight line (a radius) from the center of the cardboard to its edge. That is the path winds might follow on a stationary Earth.

3. Next, have a partner slowly turn the cardboard counter-clockwise (west to east) as seen from the North Pole. As the cardboard turns, slowly draw a straight line across its surface from the center to the edge. To be sure you move the pen along a straight line, hold a ruler or yardstick just above the cardboard. Keep the ruler fixed as you pull the pen along its side. How does this line compare with the previous one? Why is the line curved relative to the cardboard? Did it curve to the right or to the left as it moved from pole to equator?

4. Repeat the experiment, but this time draw a straight line from the edge (equator) of the circle to the center (North Pole). Again, you'll see that the line is curved and seems to bend. Did it bend toward the right or the left as it moved?

Why do the straight lines that you drew appear as curved lines on the rotating cardboard?

Winds moving across Earth's Northern Hemisphere appear to bend to the right, just as the pen did when you pulled it in a straight line across the rotating disk. In the Southern Hemisphere, the winds bend to the left. Can you explain why?

Water currents in the ocean, such as the Gulf Stream that

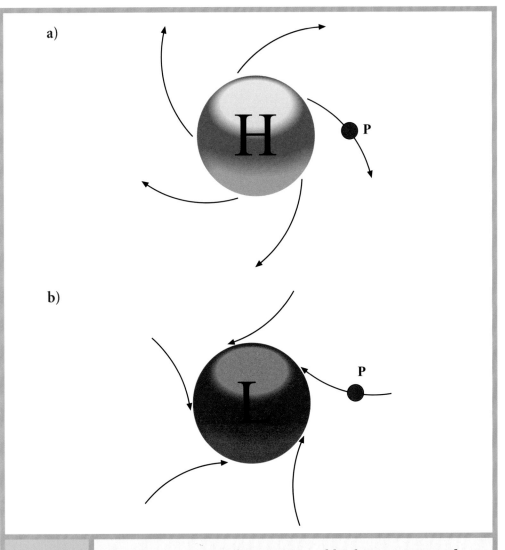

a)

b)

FIGURE

11

Wind moves away from areas of high pressure and toward areas of low pressure. Also, in the Northern Hemisphere, the rotation of Earth causes wind to move to the right. When these two factors combine, you can see that the wind at point P will move clockwise around a high-pressure system in (a) and counterclockwise around a low-pressure system in (b).

flows northward from the Gulf of Mexico, also bend due to Earth's rotation. Both winds and ocean currents bend to the right of their apparent path in the Northern Hemisphere (and to the left in the Southern Hemisphere).

Because of the Coriolis effect, as well as air pressure differences, winds in the Northern Hemisphere move clockwise about a high-pressure center and counterclockwise about a low-pressure center, as shown in Figure 11.

5. To find the direction to a high– or low-pressure center, stand with your back to the wind. Raise both arms so they are horizontal. Explain why your right hand is pointing toward higher pressure, while your left arm is pointing toward lower pressure.

IDEAS FOR A SCIENCE FAIR

- Show that winds in the Southern Hemisphere bend to the left.

- There is a belief that the Coriolis effect causes water always to turn clockwise as it enters a drain in the Northern Hemisphere, and to turn counterclockwise in drains south of the equator. Carry out experiments to test this belief.

WHAT HAPPENS WHEN AIR WARMS?

To see what happens when air warms, you can do an experiment.

1. Pull the neck of a balloon over the mouth of a clear, empty 2– or 3-liter plastic soda bottle.

2. Put a pail in a sink and fill it with hot tap water. Put the bottle in the hot water and hold it there. Watch the balloon. What happens as the temperature of the air in the bottle increases?

3. Remove the bottle and dry it.

4. Put the bottle and its attached balloon in a refrigerator. After ten minutes, look at the bottle and balloon. What happens to air when its temperature decreases?

    What do you think will happen if you place the bottle and balloon in a freezer for ten minutes? Try it! Did you predict correctly?

You Will Need

- **balloon**
- **clear, empty 2– or 3-liter plastic soda bottle**
- **pail**
- **sink**
- **hot tap water**
- **refrigerator**
- **clock or watch**
- **freezer**

IDEA FOR A SCIENCE FAIR

Design an experiment to find a mathematical relationship between the volume of a gas and its temperature. Why must you keep the pressure constant in this experiment?

GAS DENSITY AND TEMPERATURE

In Experiment 1-1, you saw that a liquid expands when heated. In this experiment, you saw that a gas, such as air, also expands when heated. Because air expands when its temperature increases, its density decreases. Density is the mass of a substance divided by its volume. When air expands, the same mass of air takes up more space. Because warm air has a larger volume than cold air, its density is less. For example, a liter (L) of air at sea-level pressure (1,013.25 mbar) and room temperature (68°F or 20°C) has a mass of 1.20 g. Its density, therefore, is

$$\frac{1.20 \text{ g}}{1.00 \text{ L}} \quad = \quad 1.20 \text{ g/L}$$

If the air is warmed to 122°F (50°C), it expands to a volume of 1.10 L. Its density, therefore, becomes

$$\frac{1.20 \text{ g}}{1.10 \text{ L}} \quad = \quad 1.09 \text{ g/L}$$

RISING, SINKING, AND DENSITY

L iquids and gases are both fluids, and, in many ways, they share similar properties. For example, both expand when heated and shrink when cooled. As you may know, a dense object, such as a stone, will sink in a less dense liquid, such as water. A stick of wood, on the other hand, floats in water because it is less dense than water.

We can use warm and cold water to model what happens when warm and cold air meet.

1. Nearly fill a clear vial or small glass with cold tap water.

2. Place a drop of blue food coloring in another vial or small glass, and then nearly fill it with hot tap water.

3. Fill an eyedropper with the colored hot water. Submerge the end of the dropper into the vial that holds the cold water. Very slowly squeeze the hot water into the cold water, as shown in Figure 12. What happens? Can you explain what you see?

4. Repeat the experiment, but this time color the cold water. Use the

You Will Need

- **2 clear vials or small glasses**
- **cold and hot tap water**
- **blue food coloring**
- **eyedropper**

clear
cold
water

hot
colored
water

| FIGURE 12 | What happens when a warm fluid meets a cold fluid? When a cold fluid meets a warm fluid? |

eyedropper to slowly squeeze the colored cold water into clear hot water. Can you predict what will happen? Try it! Were you right?

AIR MASSES AND FRONTS

An air mass is a widespread body of air that is much the same across its entire ground area. Its properties reflect the region of Earth where it forms. Air masses are classified according to where they originate: tropical (T), polar (P), and Arctic or Antarctic (A). Their moisture content is represented by continental (c) or maritime (m). Continental air masses form over land and are dry; maritime air masses form over water and are humid. When an air mass moves, it gradually changes. Air warmer than the surface over which it is moving is identified by the letter w. Air colder than the surface over which it is moving is identified by the letter k. What would be true of air masses identified by the letters cPk, mTw, cAw, mPw, and mTk?

A cold (k-type) air mass is often unstable because the cold air, warmed by the ground, rises and mixes with colder air above. A w-type air mass is more stable near the ground. The colder ground tends to keep lower air cooler than the air above. This reduces upward movement of the lower air.

Fronts form where two different air masses meet. When a cold air mass overtakes a warmer air mass, it is called a cold front. When a warm air mass overtakes a cooler air mass, it is called a warm front. A stationary front is one in which warm and cold air masses remain side-by-side in one place.

The next experiment will show you what happens when a cold front forms.

Remember, water and air are both fluids. Consequently, we can use warm and cold water to represent warm and cold air masses.

To see what happens at a cold front, prepare two or three green ice cubes to represent it. This is easily done.

1. Place two drops of green food coloring in each of three plastic medicine cups. Fill the cups with water.

2. Place the cups in a freezer until the water is frozen.

3. When the green ice cubes are available, fill a small glass with warm tap water. Add red food coloring to the water and stir until the water has a deep red color.

4. Nearly fill a clear glass loaf pan with water at room temperature.

5. Once the water in the pan stops moving, remove the green ice cubes from their

You Will Need

- **green and red food coloring**

- **3 plastic medicine cups**

- **freezer**

- **small glass**

- **warm tap water**

- **spoon**

- **clear glass loaf pan about 8 in × 5 in × 3 in deep water at room temperature**

- **cooking baster**

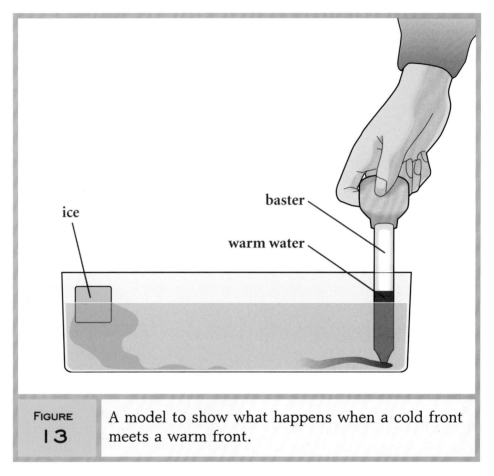

FIGURE	A model to show what happens when a cold front
13	meets a warm front.

cups. Place them in the water at one end of the pan. What happens as the ice melts?

6. After some green water collects and begins to flow horizontally, use a cooking baster to slowly add the warm red water to the bottom of the other end of the pan, as shown in Figure 13. What happens as a cold front forms? Can you explain why it happens?

ONSHORE AND OFFSHORE WINDS

On warm days, near large bodies of water, you will often find the wind blowing toward land—an onshore wind. At night, as the land cools, the wind blows toward the water—an offshore wind. An experiment will help you to see why this happens.

1. Find two identical pie pans. Pour an inch of sand into one pie pan. Pour an inch of water into the second pan.

2. Place a thermometer in each pan. Be sure the bulbs of both thermometers are submerged in the sand or water. Let both sand and water come to room temperature.

3. Then place the two pans in bright, warm sunlight, or place each pan about six inches (15 cm) beneath a 100-W light bulb.

4. In your notebook, record the temperature every five minutes for at least half an hour. The sand weighs

You Will Need

- **2 identical pie pans**
- **sand**
- **water, cold and warm**
- **2 household alcohol thermometers**
- **bright sunlight or 2 100-W light bulbs**
- **notebook**
- **pen or pencil**
- **clock or watch**

more than the water, but which warms faster—sand or water?

5. Leave the sand in place, but pour out the water. Replace the water with water that has the same, or nearly the same, temperature as the warm sand.

6. Again, record the temperature every five minutes for at least half an hour. The sand weighs more than the water, but which cools faster—sand or water?

From what you know about the density of warm air and cold air, see if you can explain onshore and offshore winds.

The weather section of your local daily newspaper probably has a weather map similar to the one in Figure 14. The map shows you the locations of high– and low-pressure centers as well as fronts, areas where precipitation can be expected, and high and low temperatures for major cities.

Look closely at the weather map. What would you expect the wind direction to be in Atlanta? In Calgary? In Miami?

Read and save the daily weather maps, and refer back to previous days' maps. In which general direction do air masses move across the United States? How can you determine the approximate speed at which a front, a high, or a low is moving across the country?

THE JET STREAM

In the Northern Hemisphere, tropical air heated by the sun rises to high altitudes and moves northward. The Coriolis effect bends it to the right, and so it becomes a west wind known as the jet stream. Its name comes from the fact that its winds are very strong (100 mph or more).

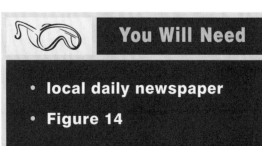

You Will Need

- **local daily newspaper**
- **Figure 14**

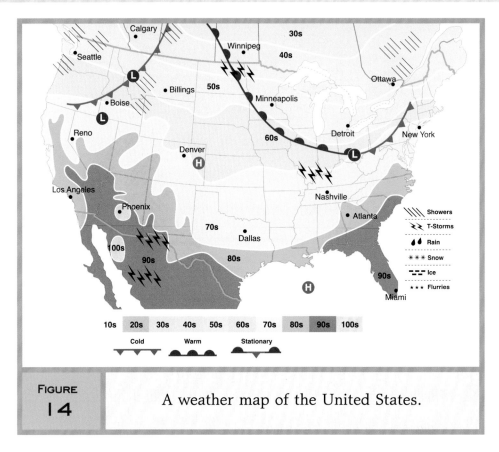

FIGURE 14

A weather map of the United States.

The jet stream forms where warm southern air meets colder air from the north at altitudes of 7 to 8 miles (11 to 13 km). It generally lies between latitudes of 35 to 60 degrees and meanders northward and southward as it travels from west to east. It has a major effect on the weather because it can steer entire weather systems. Look for the jet stream on TV weather reports or some weather maps. It is usually near the boundary between warm and cold air masses.

MAKING MORE WEATHER PREDICTIONS

From your own weather records, notes, and observations, you have probably found some clues that help you make weather forecasts. You may have discovered that clouds are valuable in predicting the weather. Here are some things that you may not have discovered.

CLOUDS AS KEYS TO FORECASTING WEATHER

Cumulus clouds are often called fair-weather clouds. However, if it is warm and humid, a cumulus cloud can grow into a cumulonimbus cloud. Violent updrafts of wind may lift the top of such a cloud to the tropopause that separates the troposphere [the lowest 6 mi (10 km)] of the atmosphere from the stratosphere. Such clouds are associated with thunderstorms.

Cirrus clouds usually appear during fair weather. However, if cirrus clouds are followed by cirrocumulus and cirrostratus clouds, a warm front may be ascending over colder air. Rain may follow within forty-eight hours. Halos of the sun or moon often appear with cirrostratus clouds. These halos can be a sign that precipitation is coming.

Dark stratus clouds form when the air is laden with moisture. If thick and heavy, they usually accompany rain or snow.

OTHER KEYS TO FORECASTING WEATHER

Barometer readings: You may have noticed that when barometer readings indicate decreasing air pressure, rain or snow often follows. Remember, low pressure means air can expand. Expanding air cools, as you learned in Experiment 2-5. Cooling can cause water vapor to condense. A rising barometric pressure is a signal that fair weather is likely to follow. Do you see why? What would you expect if your barometer readings are steady?

Cool clear nights: Cool or cold temperatures near the dew point with clear skies and little wind are accompanied by radiational cooling. Heat escapes to the upper atmosphere at night. As a result, air near the ground becomes cooler. Cool clear nights might lead you to predict dew or frost for the following morning.

Humidity: Drying air (lowering humidity) and increasing air pressure are a sign that fair weather is coming. Increasing humidity and decreasing air pressure suggest the opposite.

Fronts: Approaching cold fronts may cause brief but heavy precipitation. Warm fronts are more likely to cause precipitation that lasts longer.

As a front approaches, air pressure decreases because warm air is rising. Air pressure increases as a front passes, because the air is cooling and becoming more dense.

Warm fronts often mark the beginning of a storm and are accompanied by southerly winds. Sometimes they are preceded by fog. Cold fronts follow a storm and bring north, west, or northwest winds.

Direction of approaching weather: Weather patterns generally move from west to east. If you know the weather to your west, predict that it will reach you the next day. A front or low to your west, northwest, or southwest is likely to reach you soon. Fronts or lows to your east, southeast, or northeast will probably bypass you. Hurricanes are an exception. They move east to west across the Atlantic Ocean near the equator. They may turn northward as they approach North or Central America or as they enter the Gulf of Mexico.

Winds shifting to the north are usually followed by cooler temperatures. The opposite is true of winds shifting to the south.

Wind and air pressure: The forecasts in Table 7 are based on barometer and wind vane readings. From what you know about fronts and high and low pressure air masses, see if you can explain why these forecasts make sense.

Of course, local conditions can affect the weather. For example, northern coastal cities experience a good deal of fog. Warm moist air in contact with cold ocean water holds plenty of sea salt particles (condensation nuclei). This condition is ideal for cloud formation at ground level. Areas on the west slope of mountains often experience considerable rain, while areas east of the mountains tend to be dry. Can you explain why?

TABLE 7	Forecasts Based on Simultaneous Wind Vane and Barometer Readings	
Wind Vane Reading	**Barometer Reading**	**Forecast**
W, SW, or NW	High, rising fast	Fair and warmer, precipitation possible in 48 hours
W, SW, or NW	High, rising slowly	Fair, temperature steady for next day or two
W, SW, or NW	High, falling slowly	Fair, temperature rising slowly for next day or two
E, NE, or N	Low, falling fast	Windy, precipitation likely
S, SE, or E	Low, falling fast	Windy, precipitation likely
S or SW	Low, rising slowly	Fair, clearing if cloudy and remaining so for 48 hours
Turning to W	Low, rising fast	Clearing if cloudy, lower temperatures
SE, E, or NE	Falling slowly	Precipitation likely by next day

COMPARING FORECASTS

How do your weather forecasts compare with those made by meteorologists?

1. To find out, look at a weather map in your local newspaper each day, but don't look at the paper's weather forecast. Weather maps are based on reports from the hundreds of weather stations across North America. It is only fair that you have access to that information just as professional forecasters do.

2. Based on the weather map, your instrument readings, your notes and observations, and other things you know about the weather, make your own weather forecast for the next day. Then, and only then, compare your forecast with the paper's forecast.

You Will Need

- **weather map in local newspaper**
- **your weather instrument readings, your notes and observations**
- **newspaper and TV weather forecasts**

3. The next day, compare both forecasts with the actual weather. How well did the paper's forecaster do? How well did you do?

4. Continue making daily

forecasts. You may have found a lifelong hobby or even a future career.

5. After making your forecast, you might see what your TV meteorologist is forecasting for tomorrow. How does the TV forecast compare with the paper's forecast? How does it compare with yours?

6. Most forecasts predict the next day's high and low temperatures. You might keep a record of the predicted and the actual high and low temperatures for a month. Then plot a graph of the daily predicted and the actual high and low temperatures. How accurate were the temperature forecasts?

7. Using your records and growing weather sense, see if you can make predictions about temperature highs and lows.

IDEA FOR A SCIENCE FAIR

* Compare the accuracy of long-range TV forecasts (seven to two days in advance of the actual day) on the Weather Channel or a local station with next-day forecasts.

* How accurate are the long-range forecasts found in *The Old Farmers Almanac*?

* On a night that you are predicting dew or frost, cover one or

more plants with a light blanket or large cloth. Check your forecast the next morning. If there was dew or frost as you predicted, the plant may be free of dew or frost. Can you explain why?

WEATHER, CLIMATE, AND GLOBAL WARMING

Weather is the word we use to describe atmospheric conditions from day to day. Climate is weather in general over a long time. For example, we might say the climate of southwestern United States is hot and dry with minimal rainfall. However, a January weather report for Phoenix, Arizona, might include snow and freezing temperatures.

Scientists are concerned that Earth's overall climate is growing warmer, a condition known as global warming. About 600 million years ago, Earth's climate was very cold. Ice extended from the poles to the equator. It was also a time when there was very little carbon dioxide (CO_2) gas in the atmosphere. Earth's average temperature must have been 32°F (0°C) or colder.

Today, Earth's average temperature is 57°F (13.9°C), and the amount of carbon dioxide in the atmosphere is increasing. Prior to 1800, the concentration of carbon dioxide in the atmosphere was 280 parts per million (ppm). In other words, there were 280 molecules of carbon dioxide for every million molecules of atmosphere. Today that concentration is more than than 380 ppm. This means that more than 0.038 percent of atmospheric molecules are carbon dioxide. This is a very small quantity when you consider that oxygen makes up 21 percent of the atmosphere and nitrogen accounts for 78 percent. However, as you can see from the graph in Figure 15, the concentration of atmospheric carbon dioxide increased from 320 ppm in 1960 to 370 ppm in 2000. Its 2005 level of 380 indicates a rise of nearly 19 percent since 1960.

Scientists have examined ice cores drilled from ancient ice beds. Those cores tell us that when Earth was colder, the atmospheric carbon dioxide concentration was about 160 ppm. On the other hand, 55 million years ago Earth was very warm. Its polar ice caps had melted, and the concentration of carbon dioxide in the atmosphere was about 760 ppm.

The zigzag shape of the graph in Figure 15 is the result of summer and winter in the two hemispheres. During spring and summer in the Northern Hemisphere, atmospheric

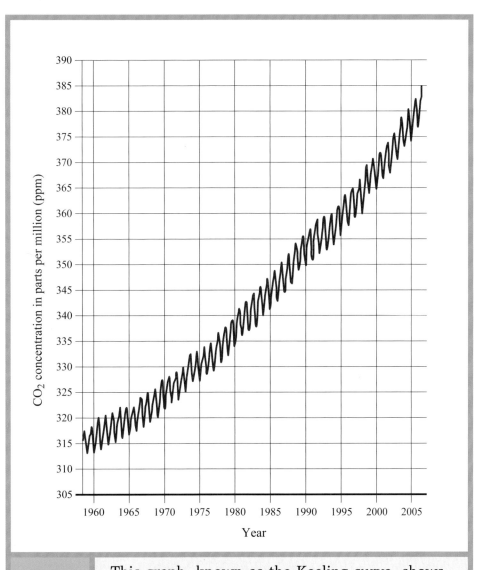

FIGURE

15

This graph, known as the Keeling curve, shows the atmospheric CO_2 concentration over time from 1958 to 2007. Measurements were made at Mauna Loa, Hawaii.

carbon dioxide decreases. The green plants and trees, in the presence of sunlight, take in the gas along with water to make starch (food) and release oxygen as a by-product. This process, known as photosynthesis, reduces the concentration of carbon dioxide in the atmosphere. During northern winters, plants are less active and the carbon dioxide level rises again.

You might ask, why doesn't the Southern Hemisphere's summer have a similar effect? If you look at a globe, you will see that Earth's land, where trees and plants grow, is predominantly north of the equator. As a result, summers south of the equator have a much smaller effect on the atmosphere's carbon dioxide level.

Carbon dioxide is one of the so-called greenhouse gases found in the atmosphere. Greenhouse gases cause global warming. Other major greenhouse gases include methane, water vapor, nitrous oxide, and chlorofluorocarbons [KLOR uh FLOR uh KAHR bunz]. Carbon dioxide, which is emitted when fossil fuels burn, is a primary human cause of global warming because it remains in the atmosphere for a very long time.

Millions of years ago, plants were abundant. These plants died and, over time, came under pressure from later plants and earth that built up over them. They slowly changed to coal, crude oil (our source of gasoline), and natural gas. These fossil fuels (so called because they are the remains of once-living plants) are a source of stored carbon—the carbon that was once in carbon dioxide. When these fossil fuels are burned in power plants, trucks, and cars, the carbon dioxide that was removed by plants eons ago is returned to the atmosphere. As Figure 15 reveals, we are adding carbon dioxide to the atmosphere faster than nature can remove it.

Every time a gallon of gasoline (assume it is octane) is burned to power a truck or car, 18 pounds (8.2 kilograms) of carbon dioxide is produced. Automobiles and light trucks in the United States consume 150 billion gallons of gasoline each year. This results in 2.7 trillion pounds (1.2 trillion kilograms) of carbon dioxide being spewed into the atmosphere. Every time a ton of coal is burned in a power plant, 3.67 tons of carbon dioxide are produced. Fossil fuels containing seven billion tons of carbon are mined or pumped from the earth every year. The burning of these fuels produces 25 billion tons of carbon dioxide.

Carbon dioxide and other greenhouse gases cause global warming. A warm Earth emits radiation (energy that is similar to light energy). The greenhouse gases in the atmosphere absorb this radiation. Then they emit their own radiation, part of which travels back to Earth. As a result, Earth is warmed by the sun and by its own atmosphere. The greater the concentration of greenhouse gases, the greater the amount of energy radiated to Earth from the atmosphere. Without the atmosphere, Earth's temperature would be about 50°F (28°C) cooler.

In the next experiment, you will make a model to show how global warming works.

Without greenhouse gases, Earth would be too cold for life. On the other hand, as the concentration of greenhouse gases increases, Earth is becoming warmer.

You can make a model of the greenhouse effect.

1. Place a household alcohol thermometer in a clear plastic container. Fold a small card to shade the thermometer bulb, as shown in Figure 16. Put the clear cover on the box. The box and its cover will serve as the Earth and its "atmosphere."

2. Put the box with the enclosed thermometer in bright sunlight.

3. Place the second thermometer beside the plastic box. Shade its bulb just as you did the other thermometer.

   Watch both thermometers for a few minutes. Is it warmer inside or outside the box?

   If you can't find a plastic

You Will Need

- **2 identical household alcohol thermometers**

- **clear plastic container that can be closed or a shoe box, plastic wrap, and tape**

- **small cards**

- **bright sunlight**

- **black construction paper**

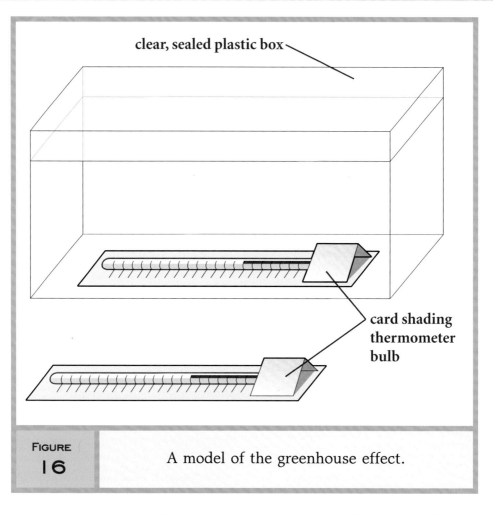

clear, sealed plastic box

card shading
thermometer
bulb

FIGURE
16

A model of the greenhouse effect.

box that can be sealed, use a shoe box. Remove its cover and

put a thermometer with a shaded bulb inside. Cover the box

with plastic wrap, seal it with tape, and place it in bright

sunlight. Place a second thermometer, with its bulb shaded,

beside the box.

Predict what you think will happen if you line the sealed

box with black paper and repeat the experiment. Try it. Was your prediction correct?

IDEAS FOR A SCIENCE FAIR

- From the tons of coal burned in the United States each year, calculate how many tons of carbon dioxide result from the burning of this coal.

- Has the increase in the cost of gasoline reduced its consumption in the United States?

MELTING ICE AND EARTH'S SEA LEVEL

O ne result of global warming may be rising sea levels. Water that is presently frozen in the seas and in glaciers resting on the ground may melt as Earth's temperature rises. In fact, many glaciers are already receding at a rapid rate. Will this melting ice raise the level of the oceans? If it does, what will happen to cities located near oceans?

An experiment will help you determine whether or not the melting of sea ice and glaciers will raise the level of the oceans.

1. Pour water into two identical drinking glasses until they are about half full.

2. To one glass add two large ice cubes. This ice represents sea ice, such as ice that floats on the Arctic Ocean. Use a marking pencil to mark the water level in the glass.

3. Place a funnel in the second glass. Mark the water level in the glass.

4. Add two large ice cubes to the funnel, as shown

You Will Need

- **2 identical drinking glasses**
- **water**
- **4 large ice cubes**
- **marking pen**
- **funnel**

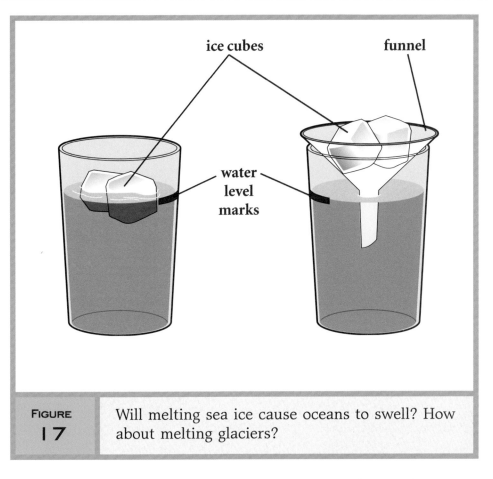

ice cubes   funnel

water
level
marks

| FIGURE 17 | Will melting sea ice cause oceans to swell? How about melting glaciers? |

in Figure 17. This ice represents the ice in glaciers that rest on land. Much of the meltwater from such glaciers will flow into rivers leading to the sea.

5. After all the ice has melted, look at the water levels in each glass. Has the water level risen in either glass?

Will melting sea ice raise the level of the oceans? How about melting glaciers on land?

GLOBAL WARMING, MELTING ICE, AND SEA LEVEL

As you saw in Experiment 4-2, melting sea ice will not change the level of the oceans. The extra volume that ice occupies when it freezes is above the water. When the ice melts, it occupies only the volume that was below the water level. However, melting glaciers that were on land add water to the oceans and raise the level of the seas.

Are all the oceans connected? Look at a globe or a map of the world to find out.

If all the Arctic sea ice were to melt, it would have no effect on sea level. However, if the Greenland glaciers melted, sea level would rise 23 feet (7 meters).

Remember Experiment 1-1 and what happens to the liquid in a thermometer when it warms. When the temperature of water rises, it expands. Consequently, there will be some rise in sea level as the seas grow warmer and take up more space. Estimates of the rise in sea level due to expansion during this century range from 4 to 8 inches (10 to 20 cm).

One place carbon dioxide is stored is in the oceans. Carbon dioxide is soluble in water. In fact, 171 cm^3 of the gas will dissolve in 100 cm^3 of cold water. But what happens when the water warms?

1. To find out, obtain two cans of cola or any carbonated beverage. Such beverages contain carbon dioxide in solution.

2. Place one can in the refrigerator for several hours; leave the other can at room temperature for the same amount of time.

3. Open the cold can. Then open the warm can. What happens to the solubility of carbon dioxide when the temperature of the water in which it is dissolved rises? How is this related to global warming?

You Will Need

- **2 cans of a carbonated beverage such as cola**

- **refrigerator**

ICY REFLECTIONS
COMPOUND GLOBAL WARMING

The loss of ice and snow from Earth's surface compounds the problem of global warming. Both ice and snow reflect sunlight. An experiment will help you see why this is a problem.

1. Place two thermometers about a foot apart on a piece of cardboard.

2. Place a heat lamp about a foot above the cardboard. Center the lamp over a point midway between the two thermometers.

3. Cover one thermometer with a sheet of black paper. Cover the other with a sheet of aluminum foil that is the same size as the black paper. Aluminum foil, like ice and snow, reflects light. Let the heat lamp shine on the two sheets for about five minutes.

4. Turn off the lamp, remove the sheets of paper and foil, and read the two thermometers. What can you conclude?

Water reflects 5 to 10 percent of the sunlight

You Will Need

- **2 household alcohol thermometers**
- **cardboard**
- **heat lamp**
- **sheet of black paper**
- **aluminum foil**
- **clock or watch**

it receives. But ice and snow reflect 80 to 90 percent of the sunlight that strikes their surfaces. As Earth's snow and ice melt, less solar energy is reflected back into space. Instead, Earth absorbs more sunlight and so is warmed even more.

EVIDENCE OF GLOBAL WARMING

Since 1900, Earth's average temperature has increased by a little more than 1°F. The concentration of carbon dioxide increased from 280 ppm to 380 ppm. Land glaciers through-out the world are shrinking as they melt. Almost all the 20 warmest years on record have occurred since 1980. Since 1950, scientists in the Northern Hemisphere have detected a general northward movement of species. They are moving northward at a rate of four miles per decade. To cope with rising temperatures, species that live on mountains have been moving upland at an average of 20 feet of altitude per decade. An advance of springlike activities of 2.3 days per decade has been noted. Plants are budding and flowering earlier. Migrating birds are arriving one to three days earlier as each decade passes. This is happening in both Europe and North America.

At Earth's polar regions, Arctic winters are 4–5°F warmer than they were 35 years ago. The extent of Arctic Ocean ice is shrinking in area. This phenomenon is believed to be related to the shrinking population of both bears and caribou.

In Antarctica, seas are warming and sea ice has been decreasing since 1950. The northern boundary of that ice has shifted southward by about 100 miles (160 km). The warmer temperatures are believed to be related to the shrinking krill population. That population is declining at the rate of 40 percent per decade. Since sea mammals feed on krill, the population of Emperor penguins has dropped by 50 percent since 1970. This is some of the evidence that reveals the existence of global warming.

Global warming can melt Earth's glaciers, raise sea levels, and flood coastal cities. As you saw in Experiment 2-6, warmer oceans increase the rate of evaporation. Adding water to the atmosphere has increased rainfall in some regions. Meanwhile, other areas, such as Africa and Australia, are feeling more intense heat and their deserts are growing. Hurricanes are fueled by warm ocean water;

consequently, warmer oceans may increase the number and severity of hurricanes.

COPING WITH GLOBAL WARMING

At the world and national level, much can be done to reduce global warming. The main goal must be to stabilize or reduce carbon dioxide levels in the atmosphere. This can be accomplished by reducing the burning of fossil fuels. It is a doable goal. By 2003, Great Britain had reduced its carbon dioxide emissions to a level 14 percent less than its 1990 emissions, and it proposes to reduce emissions by 60 percent before 2050. Governments can require automobile makers to produce cars that are more efficient—that is, cars that go farther on a gallon of gasoline. Some companies are already making hybrid cars that can go for up to 60 miles per gallon. Governments can also encourage or engage in developing and expanding mass transportation—subways, buses, trains—while encouraging people to walk or ride bikes. They can also use tax incentives or penalties to encourage the development of renewable sources of energy, while taxing companies that emit carbon dioxide.

Power plants need to move away from burning coal, oil, and natural gas to produce electrical energy. Alternative forms of energy that can be used to generate electricity include wind, solar, geothermal, tidal, wave, water, and even nuclear energy if a safe means of transporting and processing or storing nuclear waste can be developed.

What can you as one individual do to slow global warming? Here are a few things you can do, and you can probably think of others. Encourage your family to buy smaller, more efficient cars, such as hybrids. Walk, bike, or use public transportation whenever possible. Encourage and practice energy conservation. Use solar energy to heat water and, where feasible, to heat buildings. Buy only energy-efficient appliances (refrigerators, stoves, furnaces, light bulbs). Encourage towns and cities to use wind energy to power their facilities, and power companies to use wind and other renewable energy sources. If we all do our part, the effects of global warming can be lessened.

Arbor Scientific
P.O. Box 2750
Ann Arbor, MI 48106-2750
(800) 367-6695
http://www.arborsci.com

Carolina Biological Supply Co.
2700 York Road
Burlington, NC 27215-3398
(800) 334-5551
http://www.carolina.com

Connecticut Valley Biological Supply Co., Inc.
82 Valley Road, Box 326
Southampton, MA 01073
(800) 628-7748
http://www.ctvalleybio.com

Delta Education
P.O. Box 3000
80 Northwest Blvd.
Nashua, NH 03061-3000
(800) 258-1302
http://www.delta-education. com

Edmund Scientific
60 Pearce Avenue
Tonawanda, NY 14150-6711
(800) 728-6999
http://www.scientificsonline. com

Educational Innovations, Inc.
362 Main Avenue
Norwalk, CT 06851
(888) 912-7474
http://www.teachersource.com

Fisher Science Education
4500 Turnberry Drive
Hanover Park, IL 60133
(800) 955-1177
http://new.fishersci.com

Frey Scientific
P.O. Box 8101
100 Paragon Parkway
Mansfield, OH 44903
(800) 225-3739
http://www.freyscientific.com

Nasco-Fort Atkinson
P.O. Box 901
901 Janesville Avenue
Fort Atkinson, WI 53538-0901
(800) 558-9595
http://www.nascofa.com

Nasco-Modesto
P.O. Box 3837
4825 Stoddard Road
Modesto, CA 95352-3837
(800) 558-9595
http://www.enasco.com

Sargent-Welch/VWR Scientific
P.O. Box 4130
Buffalo, NY 14217
(800) 727-4368
http://www.SargentWelch.com

Science Kit & Boreal Laboratories
777 East Park Drive
P.O. Box 5003
Tonawanda, NY 14150
(800) 828-7777
http://www.sciencekit.com

Wards Natural Science
P.O. Box 92912
5100 West Henrietta Road
Rochester, NY 14692-9012
(800) 962-2660
http://www.wardsci.com

Bassett, John. *Weather and Climate*. Danbury, Conn.: Grolier Educational, 2002.

Brotak, Ed. *Wild About Weather: 50 Wet, Windy, & Wonderful Activities*. New York: Lark Books, 2004.

Breen, Mark, and Kathleen Friestad. *The Kids' Book of Weather Forecasting: Build a Weather Station, "Read" the Sky, & Make Predictions*. Nashville, Tenn.: Williamson Books, 2000.

Eubank, Mark. *The Weather Detectives: [Fun-Filled Facts, Experiments, and Activities for Kids]*. Layton, Utah: G. Smith Publisher, 2004.

Krieger, Melanie Jacobs. *How to Excel in Science Competition*. Berkeley Heights, N.J.: Enslow Publishers, Inc. 1999.

Rupp, Rebecca. *Weather*. North Adams, Mass.: Storey Publishing, 2003.

Sudipta, Bardhan-Quallen. *Championship Science Fair Projects: 100 Sure-To-Win Experiments*. New York: Sterling, 2004.

One Sky, Many Voices
http://www.ed.gov/pubs/edtechprograms/manyvoices.html

The Weather Channel
http://www.weather.com

Weather Wiz Kids
http://weatherwizkids.com